STOPPING AND SEEING

STOPPING AND SEEING

A COMPREHENSIVE COURSE IN BUDDHIST MEDITATION

Chih-i

TRANSLATED BY
THOMAS CLEARY

SHAMBHALA
Boston & London
1997

SHAMBHALA PUBLICATIONS, INC.
HORTICULTURAL HALL
300 MASSACHUSETTS AVENUE
BOSTON, MASSACHUSETTS 02115
http://www.shambhala.com

9 8 7 6 5 4 3 2 1

First Edition

Printed in Canada

♾ This edition is printed on acid-free paper that
meets the American National Standards Institute
Z39.48. Standard.

Distributed in the United States by Random House,
Inc., and in Canada by Random House of Canada Ltd.

Library of Congress Cataloging-in-Publication Data

Chih-i, 538–597.
[Mo ho chih kuan. English. Selections]
Stopping and seeing: a comprehensive course in Buddhist
meditation/Chih-i; translated by Thomas Cleary.
p. cm.
ISBN 1-57062-275-2 (alk. paper)
1. T'ien-t'ai Buddhism—Doctrines—Early works to 1800.
2. Meditation—xT'ien-t'tai Buddhism—Early works to 1800.
3. Samatha (Buddhism)—Early works to 1800. 4. Vipaśyanā
(Buddhism)—Early works to 1800. I. Title.
BQ9149.C454M6213 1997

CONTENTS

TRANSLATOR'S INTRODUCTION

"STOPPING" AND "SEEING" ARE THE YIN AND YANG of Buddhist meditation, complementary twin halves of a unified whole. The fundamental meaning of "stopping and seeing," sometimes more solemnly called cessation and contemplation, is stopping delusion and seeing truth. All Buddhist meditations, and indeed all Buddhist principles and practices, can be categorized and organized in terms of stopping, seeing, and the integration of stopping and seeing.

There are a number of books on stopping and seeing written in Chinese. The most comprehensive of these is called *Mo-ho Chih-kuan*, or *Great Stopping and Seeing*, a record of lectures on Buddhist meditation by the great T'ien-t'ai master Chih-i, who lived in the sixth century.

Great Stopping and Seeing is one of the so-called Three Great Works of T'ien-t'ai Buddhism, which all apprentices of that school educated in the traditional manner are expected to work through in the course of a twelve-year period of learning and practice.

Great Stopping and Seeing is also a traditional source-book for Zen and Pure Land Buddhism. Both Zen and

Pure Land Buddhism were intimately connected with T'ien-t'ai Buddhism in their early stages of development, and contact was renewed at various points in history, not only in China but also in Korea and Japan. The T'ien-t'ai patriarch Chih-i appears as a Zen master in Zen literature, and as a Pure Land patriarch in Pure Land literature.

Chih-i lived from 538 to 597 of the common era. His father, whose surname was Ch'en, was from an old family of Confucian scholars, distinguished in public service for generations. His mother was from the Hsu clan, which was deeply involved in Taoism and produced many distinguished figures in that discipline. The inclusion of Taoist medical doctrines and practices in Chih-i's work on Buddhist meditation probably reflects his early education within the family context.

Chih-i was inspired as a child by hearing recitation of Buddhist scripture, which seemed inexplicably familiar to him. When he was fifteen years old, he determined to enter religious orders, leaving behind the political or military career Confucian men of leading families were ordinarily expected to pursue. His parents would not permit his ordination, and he formally became a Buddhist novice only after they passed away when he was eighteen years old.

Fully ordained at the age of twenty after a two-year novitiate, Chih-i spent the next twenty years reciting scriptures and studying the whole Buddhist canon. He also practiced repentance rituals, which are supposed to purify the mind of stultifying accretions and adhesions of mundane habit. Rewarded for his efforts with beatific visions as depicted in the scriptures, Chih-i was now constantly rapt in meditation.

Satisfied for a time with his experiences, Chih-i no longer felt the need to seek advice from anyone. This changed when the meditation master Hui-ssu (514–577) appeared.

It is said that Hui-ssu had foreseen the persecution of Buddhism that was to take place in northern China in the 570s and was heading for the sacred Mount Heng, the southern of the five sacred mountains of traditional China. He and Chih-i met on a mountain in what is now Hunan, where Hui-ssu had stopped on his way.

Completing his studies under the guidance of Hui-ssu, Chih-i took his leave in 569 and went to Chin-ling (present-day Nanking), where he began to teach. In 575 he left his followers, for unspecified reasons, and went into seclusion on Mount T'ien-t'ai, "Terrace of Heaven," located in Chekiang province on the eastern seaboard of China. There Emperor Hsuan of the Ch'en dynasty, who was a clansman of the master, had a monastery built for him, assigning the tax revenues of a considerable area to its upkeep. It is from this mountain that the T'ien-t'ai school gets its name.

The Ch'en dynasty was destroyed in 588 by the Sui dynasty, under which China was reunified after centuries of division into Turkic and Chinese empires. Imperial patronage of Chih-i and his T'ien-t'ai school continued, nevertheless. The first emperor of the new dynasty, a devotee of Buddhism, requested and received the bodhisattva precepts and a religious name from Chih-i, and in turn bestowed on the teacher an honorific title, Chih-che, "the Wise One," by which he is also commonly known. Chih-i spent the rest of his life teaching on Mount T'ien-t'ai, and his lectures, recorded and compiled by his foremost disciple, became one of the most important resources of East Asian Buddhism.

The vast quantity and range of Indian and Central Asian Buddhist literature translated into Chinese, originating from different communities and formulated at different times, confronted the Chinese Buddhists with the monumental problem of organizing, systematizing, and synthesizing this material. Each of the major schools of Chinese Buddhism developed its own method of classifying the teachings, and the T'ien-t'ai school of Chih-i features one of the most elaborate schemes of theoretical and practical syncretism, based on the times, methods, and levels of meaning of the various doctrines.

For the purposes of stopping and seeing, Chih-i's classification of Buddhist teachings centers on four levels of doctrine, referred to as the Three Baskets teaching, the common teaching, the separate teaching, and the complete teaching. The Three Baskets teaching refers to what is often called the Hinayana or Small Vehicle, which focuses on individual liberation. The common teaching refers to the doctrine of emptiness, which pervades all the teachings, although it is implicit in some and explicit in others. The separate teaching is so called because it is special in that it is only for greathearted bodhisattvas, who work for the welfare, liberation, and enlightenment of all beings. The complete teaching deals with universal Buddha-nature and the attainment of all knowledge.

Chih-i presents these four levels of teaching in terms of four kinds of four truths. The four truths, generally speaking, are the foundations of Buddhism: the truth of suffering, the truth of the cause of suffering, the truth of the end of suffering, and the truth of the path to the end of suffering. The Three Baskets teaching deals with what Chih-i calls the four truths of birth and death, or the four truths of samsara. The common teaching deals with what he calls the birthless four truths, which pertain to the state of realization of nirvana and emptiness. The separate teaching deals with what Chih-i calls the infinite four truths, in which the bodhisattva confronts the unlimited differentiations in the four truths according to the infinite differences in beings. The complete teaching deals with what he calls the inconceivable four truths, which pertain to the perception and understanding of Buddhahood. These four kinds of four truths are all defined in the text of *Great Stopping and Seeing*.

While Chih-i also defines several formats of meditation in considerable detail—sitting, walking, half walking and half sitting, and neither walking nor sitting—these are nevertheless still generalities, which have been modified from time to time, not only in the specialized Pure Land and Zen schools, but also within the T'ien-t'ai school itself.

The sitting style is common in Zen, the walking style is common in Pure Land, the half-walking-and-half-sitting style is common in Esoteric Buddhism, and the neither-walking-nor-sitting style is also common in traditional Zen. Each of the four formats, nevertheless, can be found in all these schools, although not necessarily at the same time. Of these four, the one that is accessible to lay people without necessitating any formal apparatus, schedule, or special environment is the last one, which is also called "according to one's own mentation." This style, which actually includes sitting, walking, and meditation in all activities and under all circumstances, has been particularly recommended by Zen masters since the eleventh century, with the decline of institutionalized Buddhism.

This volume presents a translation of the first quarter of Chih-i's monumental *Mo-ho Chih-kuan,* which covers the principles and methods of Buddhist meditation from the first inspiration of the thought of enlightenment to the inclusion of all Buddhist teachings within stopping and seeing. This part of the text also describes the bases of Pure Land meditation, Insight meditation, and Zen meditation, as well as the foundations of symbolic Esoteric meditation rites. As such, it has been a perennial source-book and treasury of teachings for Buddhists of all schools for fourteen hundred years.

STOPPING AND SEEING

1

FIRST I WILL EXPLAIN THE GREAT MEANING, wrap up the beginning and end, cap the start and finish. The meaning is broad and hard to see; now I will treat it in terms of five aspects: awakening the great mind, cultivating the great practice, experiencing the great result, rending the great net, and returning to the great abode.

What is awakening the great mind? People are ignorant and deluded, although unaware of it themselves; we urge them to wake up, seeking enlightenment above and edifying others below.

What is cultivating the great practice? Although we have aroused our determination, if we just look down the road and do not move, we will never arrive. So we diligently practice four kinds of concentrated meditation with steadfast and powerful vigor.

What is realizing the great result? Although we do not seek pure heaven, heaven naturally responds, telling of sublime rewards, comforting and gladdening the mind.

What is rending the great net? The various scriptures and treatises open people's eyes, yet they cling to one and doubt another, affirm one and deny others. When they hear that milk is like snow [in that it is white], they think that means it is cold. When they hear that milk is like a crane [in that it is white], they think that means it moves. Here I will synthesize the scriptures and treatises, untie knots and free them from this trap.

What is returning to the great abode? The truth has no beginning or end, no passage or blockage. If one knows the realm of reality, it has no beginning or end, no passage or blockage; one's mind will open up with great clarity and be unobstructed and free.

First I will deal with the question of awakening the great mind. [The term for the mind of enlightenment in Sanskrit is *bodhichitta*:] *Bodhi* (meaning enlightenment) is called the Path in Chinese. *Chitta* means mind, referring to the mind that thinks and knows. The term *path* also has general and particular meanings. They may be analyzed into ten overall categories.

If the mind is continually covetous, angry, and deluded, impossible to control or clear out, increasingly so as time goes on, one produces the worst kind of evils. This is arousing the hellish mind, traveling on the path of fire.

If the mind keeps thinking of desire to have many subordinates, like a sea drinking rivers, like a fire burning kindling, one produces middling evils. This is arousing the mind of animality, traveling on the path of blood.

If the mind keeps thinking of desire for fame and praise, vainly wanting to be compared to sages without any true inner worth, one creates lesser evils. This is arousing the ghostly mind, traveling the path of swords.

If the mind continually wants to be better than others and cannot bear to be less than others, one slights others and esteems oneself, like an owl flying high looking down, while outwardly extolling humanity, righteousness, etiquette, knowledge, and faithfulness. One then develops the lowest kind of good mind and travels the path of titans.

If the mind continually longs for worldly comfort, to rest the stinking body and delight the ignorant mind, then one develops the middling kind of good mind and travels the path of humans.

If the mind continually realizes that pain is predominant in the paths of hell, animals, and ghosts, and that pain and pleasure are mixed in the human realm, while heaven is pure pleasure, one bars the senses so they don't go out and sense data don't enter. Then one develops the superior kind of good mind and travels the path of heaven.

If the mind continually wants power, so that all go along with whatever one does, says, or thinks, this is arousing the mind of the commander of the realm of desire, traveling on the path of the murderer.

If the mind continually wants intellectual knowledge and brilliance, this is arousing the mind of worldly knowledge, traveling on the path of philosophers.

If the mind is only slightly covered by the outward enjoyment of sense data and desires, and the bliss of the first three stages of meditation is like a spring emerging from rock, with inner bliss predominant, this is arousing the devout mind and traveling the path of pure form and formlessness.

If the mind is constantly aware that ordinary people obsessively sink into the circle of good and bad, while sages repudiate it, and that destroying evil depends on pure wisdom, that pure wisdom comes from pure meditation, and that pure meditation proceeds from pure discipline, and thus values wisdom, meditation, and discipline as the hungry and thirsty value food and drink, this is arousing the untainted mind, traveling the path of the two vehicles of individual liberation.

There are many things wrong with these minds and paths. I just briefly mention ten as a summary. Sometimes the upper ones are divided and the lower ones combined, sometimes the lower ones are divided and the upper ones combined. I just make the number ten stand for the totality.

I bring up an individual type as a point of departure to talk about. The one that is strongest will pull you first. As a treatise says, "The immoral mind falls into hell, the covetous mind degenerates into a hungry ghost, the shameless mind degenerates into an animal." That is what this means.

Sometimes one first produces a wrong mind, or one may first produce a right mind; sometimes right and wrong arise simultaneously. This is likened to elephants, fish, and wind all making the water of a lake turbulent. Elephants symbolize the external, fish symbolize the internal, and wind symbolizes the simultaneous occurrence of both. Elephants also symbolize errors occurring externally, fish symbolize weakness of inner contemplation, being stirred by the two extremes, and wind symbolizes inside and outside mixing together, polluted, turbulent, and confused.

Also, the first nine of the aforementioned ten types of mind are in the province of birth and death, like caterpillars binding themselves. The last one is in the province of nirvana, like an antelope bounding alone; although such people manage to liberate themselves, they have not yet fulfilled Buddhahood. Therefore I weed out both the first nine and the last one because both are wrong. The first nine are mundane, neither moving nor getting out; as for the last one, although such people get out, they lack great compassion. Both are wrong, so I eliminate both.

Also like this are various facets of doctrine such as compounded and uncompounded, tainted and untainted, good and bad, defiled and pure, bondage and liberation, real and conventional.

Furthermore, the first nine paths involve the truth of suffering in the world. As for the last one, although it is not the truth of suffering, nevertheless it is still roundabout, crude, nihilistic, and shallow. So both the first nine and the last one are wrong, and I therefore eliminate them.

Next, the terms *compounded* and *tainted* are used in reference to the truth of accumulation of suffering. The last path is not the truth of accumulation, but even so it is roundabout, crude, nihilistic, and shallow. Again I eliminate both the first nine and the last one as wrong.

Next, the definitions *good and bad* and *defiled and pure* are used in connection with the truth of the path to end suffering. The last path is the truth of the path to end suffering, but even so I eliminate it as before.

Next, the terms *bondage and liberation* and *real and conventional* are used in reference to the truth of extinction of suffering. Although the last path is the truth of extinction, as before I eliminate it.

If you understand this, then carry on this examination in all your senses, sense experiences, deeds, words, and thoughts, in all activities, whenever the mind acts and thinks; do not let polluted states of mind arise, or if they arise, then extinguish them right away. Just as someone with clear vision can avoid a dangerous road, there are intelligent people in the world who can avoid what is bad. If beginning practitioners can see the meaning of this, they can be a reliance for the world.

QUESTION: Do practitioners inspire their own minds, or do others induce their inspiration?

ANSWER: It has nothing to do with self and others; it is just a matter of inspiration of the mind through response to an inner sense of contact with truth. It is like when a child falls into water or fire its parents will frantically rush to save it. The *Pure Name Scripture* says, "When a child gets sick, the parents get sick too." The *Great Perfect Nirvana Scripture* says, "Parents are most concerned about an ailing child." To move the mountain of the nature of reality and enter the ocean of birth and death, there is the "sickness practice" [identifying with the bad] and the "childlike practice" [identifying with the good].

A meditation scripture says, "Buddha teaches based on four accords: according to inclinations, according to situations, according to remedy, and according to beneficial meaning." The Buddha teaches people so as to help and protect their minds and make them happy, applying the teaching to their predilections to make it easy for them to take up practice, observing the seriousness of the illness to prescribe the appropriate dosage of medicine. When the potential for the Path becomes ripe with time, one awakens to the Path when hearing about it. Is this not the benefit of response to inner sense according to potential?

In terms of the four aims according to the *Treatise on Transcendent Wisdom*, the differentiation of mundane phenomena is called the aim of the world; adapting to capabilities is called the aim of helping people. These two aims are the same as the four accords. This too is response to inner sense.

Furthermore, to cite the five reasons given in the treatise for expounding the scriptures on transcendent wisdom, they are as follows: first, to explain the various practices of enlightening beings; second, to cause enlightening beings to increase absorption in remembrance of Buddha; third, to explain the characteristics of nonregression; fourth, to remove the disciples' faults and errors; and fifth, to explain the ultimate truth. These are the reasons for the discourses of the scriptures on transcendent wisdom.

These five reasons, the four accords, and the four aims are not different from each other, and they are also the same as the five causes of expounding the scriptures on transcendent wisdom. If an explanation is not adjusted to people's potentials, it will trouble them, and so be of no benefit to them. But if one showers great compassion, it will be possible to proceed from vagueness to clarity.

It says in the treatise, "A true teaching, an exponent, and an audience are hard to find." Birth and death neither has extremes nor has no extremes; the character of reality is neither hard nor easy, neither existent nor nonexistent: this is called a true teaching, and those who can teach it and hear it are called true exponents and audience. Having the benefit of the first three aims (of the world, for helping people, and curing) is called the extreme of existence; having the benefit of ultimate truth is called neither the extreme of existence nor the extreme of nonexistence. Therefore one can accomplish the great matter by knowing interdependent origination. This is the meaning of response to inner sense.

So the four accords, four aims, and five reasons are different in name but the same in meaning. Now I will explain this. The four accords are the benefit of response of great compassion, the four aims are the universal giving of pity; this amounts to the difference between right and left, that is all. As for the causes, sometimes the cause is based on the holy relative to the ordinary; sometimes it is based on the ordinary relative to the holy. Therefore inner sense and response interact.

Know that the three principles (of the four accords, four aims, and five causes) accord in word and experience, so their meanings are the same. Accord with inclinations concentrates on telling what is valued in cultivating cause; the aim of the world concentrates on telling the differences in consequences. Here there is only a matter of the difference of cause and effect. Accord with situations picks out principles to apply to the person; the aim of helping the person means observing the person in order to set forth an appropriate teaching. Here there is the difference of inclination and response.

Also, in reference to the five causes, with people's inclinations as the cause, Buddha explains one principle as all principles, this being the inspiration for great enlightenment. In terms of the scripture, this is accord with inclinations; in terms of the treatise, this is the aim of the world. If people have great energy and courage, Buddha explains one practice as all practices, namely the four concentrations. In terms of the scripture, this is accord with situations; in terms of the treatise, this is the aim of helping people.

If people have universally impartial wisdom, or the knowledge of universal equality, as the cause, they experience the Buddha explaining one refutation refuting everything, and attain a superlative effect as a consequence, comprehending the scriptures and treatises. In terms of both the scripture and the treatise this is a curative. People with the eye of enlightened knowledge as the cause experience the Buddha explaining the ultimate of one as the ultimate of all, and can explain silent extinction, the ultimate essence. In both the scripture and the treatise this is the ultimate truth.

Also in reference to the five causes and five reasons, the determination for enlightenment is the root of all practices. Mention of various practices in the treatise is just a matter of the difference between the branches and the roots, that is all. The four concentrations are general practices, and the remembrance of Buddha is a specialized practice; this is merely the difference between the general and the specialized.

In reference to higher rewards, there is full explanation of the objective and subjective rewards, of the fruits of practice and the fruits of reward, whereas in reference to nonregression there is only mention of the characteristics of the fruits of practice and the entering of those states; this is only a matter of the difference of being twofold or simplex.

In reference to removal of doubts and sticking points on the scriptures and treatises, scriptures and treatises are the object of doubt and clinging. As for removal of the faults of disciples, this refers to the person who creates errors. Here there is only the difference of person and object. The ultimate consummation of beginning and end can easily be seen to be synonymous with the absolute truth; the reason they are not different is that the meaning is the same.

Also, the sages speak in many ways: sometimes in order, sometimes not in order; sometimes fully, sometimes not fully; sometimes mixed, sometimes not mixed. The four aims may fulfill the five causes, and the five causes may fulfill the four aims; sometimes the four aims all fulfill one cause, or one cause fulfills one aim. Or each cause may contain all four aims, and the four aims may contain the five causes. Thus they mutually fulfill and reveal each other in various ways. After all, they are wrapped up in three cessations and contemplations, which can be known by the meaning. They are also wrapped up in one cessation and one contemplation: the determination for enlightenment is contemplation; the stopping of the errant, biased mind is cessation.

In revealing what is right, there are three more meanings: first, the four truths; next, the four universal vows; finally, the six identities.

The names and characteristics of the four truths appear in the book on holy practices in the major scripture: they are birth and death, birthless, infinite, and uncreate.

In the four truths of birth and death, suffering and its cause are mundane cause and effect; the Way and extinction are transmundane cause and effect. Suffering refers to the changes of birth, aging, and death. The cause is the movement of the four mental torrents [opinions, desires, objects, becoming]. The Way consists of curative measures to avert and remove these. Extinction is extinguishing their existence and returning them to nonexistence. In this case, both the mundane and the transmundane involve change, so these are called the four truths of birth and death.

In the birthless four truths, there is no oppression in suffering; all is empty. How can there be emptiness that can get rid of emptiness? Matter itself is empty, and so are sensations, perceptions, conditioning, and consciousness; therefore there is no sign of oppression. The cause has no sign of combination; cause and effect are both empty. How can there be emptiness of cause and emptiness of effect combining? This applies to all desire, anger, and delusion. The Way has no duality; there is no curative and nothing cured. Since there is no one in emptiness, how could there be two? Since things are originally not so, they do not now die out. Not so, no extinction; these are called the birthless four truths.

In the infinite four truths, when distinctly enumerated, suffering has infinite forms. Even in one state of existence there are numerous kinds of suffering; how much more in the ten states of existence. These are beyond the scope of knowledge or perception of those in the two vehicles; only enlightening beings can comprehend them. For example, in the hells there are various different kinds of suffering: being skinned, dismembered, burned, cut, and so on. They are countless, as are indeed those of other states as well, considering their various bodies, senses, perceptions, conditionings, and consciousnesses. It would be easier to count particles of dust, grains of sand, or drops of water in the ocean. This is why they cannot be known or seen by those of the two vehicles; only the eye of knowledge of enlightening beings can comprehend them.

There are also countless forms of the cause of suffering; the variety of covetous, spiteful, and deluded acts of mind, body, and speech. When the body is bent, the shadow is crooked; when the voice is loud, the echo is muddled. Enlightening beings are unerringly aware of this.

The Way also has infinite forms: analysis and comprehension, crude and refined techniques, indirect and direct, long and short, temporary and true. Enlightening beings understand them precisely, without confusion.

Extinction also has infinite characteristics; certain methods can extinguish views, certain methods can extinguish rumination, each method having a number of principal and auxiliary techniques. Enlightening beings see these clearly without any error.

Also, the multitude of principal and auxiliary techniques, being identical to emptiness, have no multiplicity, but even though they have no multiplicity, enlightening beings distinguish them severally without error or confusion. Certain techniques can extinguish the four basic afflictions by analysis; certain techniques can extinguish the four basic afflictions by comprehension; certain techniques can extinguish the delusions which are numerous as particles of dust and grains of sand; certain techniques can extinguish ignorance. Various and numerous as they are, each is distinct.

Also, there is multiplicity because of the distinctions in the first three aims, while there is no multiplicity in terms of the aim of ultimate truth. Although there is no plurality, because we discuss them in terms of multiplicity, we call these the infinite four truths.

In the uncreate four truths, all is reality, inconceivable. It is not only in ultimate truth that there is no plurality; there is no plurality in the other three aims, or indeed in all things. The meaning of this is obvious and need not be written down in detail.

If we set up a vertical correspondence of the four truths with the four lands, there is increase and decrease. In the land of common abode, there are four truths; in the expedient land, there are three; in the land of true reward, there are two; in the land of silent light, there is only one. To align them horizontally, in the common abode, there are the truths of birth and death; in the expedient land, there is no birth and death; in the land of true reward, there are the infinite truths; in the land of silent light, there are the uncreate truths.

Also, when spoken of as a whole they are called the four truths, while when spoken of specifically they are called the twelve conditions. "Suffering" comprises seven of these twelve elements: discriminating consciousness, name and form, sense media, contact, sensation, birth, old age and death. The "cause of suffering" comprises five of the twelve elements: ignorance, conditioning, craving, grasping, and becoming. "The Way" consists of expedients for quelling these causal relations. "Extinction" is the extinction of ignorance and the rest of the twelve, including old age and death.

Therefore the major scripture elaborates four sets of four truths and four sets of twelve conditions. Those of lesser wisdom gain the enlightenment of listeners by contemplating them; those of middling wisdom gain the enlightenment of individual illuminates by contemplating them. Those of superior wisdom gain the enlightenment of enlightening beings by contemplating them; those of supreme wisdom gain the enlightenment of Buddhas by contemplating them.

Also, a verse on the Middle Way says,

> *Phenomena produced by conditions*
> *I say are empty.*
> *This too I call artificial description,*
> *And the meaning of the Middle Way.*

"Phenomena produced by conditions" refers to birth and death; "I say are empty" refers to birthlessness and deathlessness. "This too I call artificial description" refers to the infinite; "and the meaning of the Middle Way" refers to the uncreate. We can also interpret thus: "conditions" are "the cause of suffering," "that which is produced" is "suffering." The techniques for extinguishing suffering are "the Way," and the end of suffering and its cause is "extinction."

Also, when the verse says "conditions," this refers to ignorance; "phenomena produced" refers to conditioning, name and form, the sense media, and so forth. Therefore it is written that the birthless and deathless aspect of the twelve conditions is explained for sharp disciples, while the born and dying aspect of the twelve conditions is explained for dull disciples. One should know that the totalistic explanation of this verse of the *Treatise on the Middle Way* is the four kinds of four truths; and the particularized explanation is the four kinds of twelve conditions.

The scriptures speak of various ways of arousing the aspiration for enlightenment. They speak of arousing the aspiration for enlightenment by thinking of various principles or by observing various characteristics of Buddha or by witnessing various spiritual displays or by hearing various doctrines or by traveling in various lands or by observing various groups or by seeing various practices cultivated or by seeing various things perish or by seeing various errors or by seeing others suffer various pains. These are cited in brief as ten main ways, but there are more.

As for arousing the aspiration by thinking of principle, the nature of things is naturally so—cause cannot defile it, suffering cannot torment it, the Way cannot reach it, extinction cannot purify it. Just as clouds enveloping the moon cannot hinder or harm it, once afflictions are removed, one sees the nature of things. Scripture says, "Extinction is not the real truth; by extinction we meet with reality." Since even extinction is not the real truth, how could the other three truths be the real truth? There is no enlightenment in afflictions, there are no afflictions in enlightenment. This is called arousing the aspiration for enlightenment by thinking of the four truths of birth and death, seeking Buddhahood above and teaching people below.

As for arousing the aspiration by thinking of the birthless four truths, the nature of things is not different from suffering and its cause; it is just because of misunderstanding suffering and its cause that one loses sight of the nature of things. It is like water freezing into ice—there is no separate water. When one realizes that in suffering and its cause there is no suffering or cause, then one understands the nature of things. Since even suffering and its cause are it, needless to say so are the Way and extinction. Scripture says, "Afflictions are enlightenment, enlightenment is the afflictions." This is called arousing the aspiration for enlightenment by thinking of the birthless four truths, seeking above and teaching below.

As for thinking of the infinite four truths, the nature of things is called the character of reality; it is not the sphere of the two vehicles, much less of ordinary people. Beyond the two extremes there is a distinct pure truth. This is called arousing the aspiration by thinking of the infinite four truths, seeking above and teaching below.

As for thinking of the uncreate, the nature of things and all things are not two, not different. Even the ordinary state is it, how much more so the two vehicles. To seek the character of reality outside of ordinary things is like running from the space in one place to look for space elsewhere. The ordinary is the true; there is no need to abandon the ordinary and strive for the holy. Scripture says, "Life and death is nirvana; each form, each scent, is all the Middle Way." This is called arousing the aspiration for enlightenment by thinking of the uncreate four truths, seeking above and teaching below.

If, thinking one principle through, you are clear about the entire cosmos, comprehending its bounds, arriving at its depths, thoroughly investigating horizontally and vertically, including phenomena and noumena, seeking above and teaching below, that can be called arousing the aspiration for enlightenment. Enlightenment is called the Way, and the Way can reach the horizontal and vertical Other Shore; this is called the consummation of the aspiration. Therefore we have made the distinctions of shallowness and depth all in thinking of principle, the phenomena and noumenon all-pervasive; this will apply to each method we discuss from here on.

As for arousing the aspiration by observing the marks of distinction and embellishments of Buddha, seeing the features of the mortal body of Buddha clearly manifest, clearly apprehending where they are, radiant, beautiful, shining brightly, impossible to fabricate, surpassing the marks of distinction on a universal ruler, which are rare in the world, realizing there is none in heaven or on earth equal to Buddha, none comparable in the worlds of the ten directions, if one aspires to equal the Buddha and liberate countless beings, this is arousing the aspiration for enlightenment by viewing the marks and embellishments of the adaptive embodiment of Buddha, seeking above and teaching below.

If, seeing Buddha, one knows there is no Buddha in Buddha, if, seeing Buddha's marks and embellishments, one knows marks and embellishments are not marks and embellishments, and knows that Buddha and the marks are like space, and in space there is no Buddha, much less any marks and embellishments, then, seeing Buddha is not Buddha, one sees Buddha, and seeing the marks are not marks, one sees the marks, and aspires to equal Buddha and liberate countless sentient beings, this is arousing the aspiration for enlightenment by seeing marks and embellishments of the higher adaptive embodiment of Buddha, seeking above and teaching below.

Suppose one sees the physical characteristics of Buddha manifesting everything, like seeing images of myriad forms in a clear mirror; neither ordinary people nor sages can find the bounds of each individual mark and embellishment. Even the god Brahma cannot see the top of Buddha's head, even the magically gifted saint Maudgalyayana could not thoroughly comprehend Buddha's voice. The treatisesays, "The formless supreme body is not adorned by adornments." Seeing Buddha in this way and aspiring to equal Buddha is arousing the aspiration for enlightenment by seeing the marks and embellishments of the Buddha of reward, seeking above and teaching below.

If one sees the Buddha and knows that the Buddha's knowledge is profound and comprehends the characteristics of evil and good, illuminating everywhere, and one knows that the subtle pure reality body of Buddha is replete with thirty-two marks, each mark and embellishment being identical to features of reality, and one knows that the cosmos of reality is complete and undiminishing, and one thus aspires to attain Buddhahood and equal the Buddha, this is arousing the aspiration for enlightenment by seeing the marks and embellishments of the reality-body Buddha, seeking above and teaching below.

What is arousing the aspiration for enlightenment by seeing the Buddha's various spiritual displays? One may aspire to attain Buddhahood on seeing the Buddha absorbed in making one display by means of a basic meditation state, so that one does not sense multiplicity, radiating a light, for example, that shines brightly from the lowest hell to the highest heaven so that sky and earth are clearly illumined and the sun and the moon and the stars become invisible.

Or one might aspire to attain Buddhahood on seeing Buddha responding to all people without duality, based on the Buddha's birthless noumenon, able to cause each individual to see the Buddha before him or her alone.

Or one might aspire to Buddhahood on seeing Buddha sit, walk, stand, and recline in countless worlds in the ten directions without movement in the real nature, based on absorption in the matrix of realization of thusness.

Or one might aspire to Buddhahood on seeing Buddha as nondual, not different from the spiritual displays; the Buddha makes the spiritual displays, the spiritual displays make the Buddha. As neutral creations of creations, the creations make further creations, ad infinitum, all inconceivable, all being aspects of reality doing the work of Buddhas.

What about aspiring to Buddhahood on hearing various doctrines? One might hear the one phrase "birth and death" from a Buddha or a teacher or a scripture, and thereupon understand that mundane and transmundane phenomena are continuously being renewed, being born and perishing, changing from moment to moment, and that discipline, wisdom, liberation, and tranquillity are real, and then aspire to become a Buddha and be able to explain the path of purity.

Or one might hear of birth and death and understand that the four truths are all unborn and unperishing. There are no thorns in the void, so how can they be extracted? Who suffers, who causes suffering, who cultivates the Way, who realizes extinction? Ultimately pure, subject and object are quiescent. Based on this understanding, one may aspire to Buddhahood to be able to explain the path of purity.

Or one might hear of birth and death and understand that birth and death as opposed to nonbirth and nondeath is dualistic, and that neither birth and death nor nonbirth and nondeath is the Middle Way. The Middle Way is pure and unique, going beyond both the birth-death cycle and nirvana. Based on this understanding, one may aspire to Buddhahood to be able to explain the supreme Way, emerging alone like a lotus coming out of the water, like the moon in the sky.

Or one may hear of birth and death and understand that birth and death, nonbirth and nondeath, and neither birth and death nor nonbirth and nondeath simultaneously illumine birth and death and nonbirth and nondeath, understanding that one is three and the three are one, realizing the mystic permanence and bliss of the reality realm is complete therein. With this understanding, one may aspire to attain Buddhahood to expound the esoteric treasury, like a man of virtue taking a stone and making it a jewel, taking poison and making it medicine.

One may hear of the birthless and take it that the two vehicles have no birth in the triple world, while enlightening beings are not yet birthless. One may hear of the birthless and take it that all three vehicles have no birth in the triple world. One may hear of the birthless and take it to apply only to enlightening beings, not to the two vehicles; enlightening beings first have no individual birth, then no transformational birth. One may hear of the birthless and take it that as one is unborn, all are unborn.

The same patterns apply to hearing about the infinite. One may hear of the infinite and construe the methods of the two vehicles—the four truths, the sixteen truths, and so on—as infinite. One may hear of the infinite and take it that the two vehicles use it themselves to subdue delusion but cannot teach others, while enlightening beings use this infinite to get rid of their own delusions and also to teach others. One may hear of the infinite and take it to apply only to enlightening beings, not to the two vehicles, and take it that enlightening beings use it both to annihilate inner multifarious delusions and also to subdue outer multifarious delusions. One may hear of the infinite and take it to apply only to enlightening beings, and take it that they use it to annihilate both inner and outer multifarious delusions and also to subdue ignorance.

The same patterns apply to hearing about the uncreate. One may hear of the uncreate and construe it as uncreated by Buddha, gods, people, or titans, and take it that the two vehicles realize this uncreate. The *Scripture on Consideration of Benefit* says, "We study the uncreate and have realized it, while enlightening beings cannot realize it." One may hear of the uncreate and take it that the three vehicles all can realize it. One may hear of the uncreate and take it that it is not the sphere of the two vehicles, much less that of ordinary people, that enlightening beings break through the provisional uncreate and realize the true uncreate. One may hear of the uncreate and take it to mean realizing the true uncreate in the provisional uncreate.

If one gets the meaning of this, then whatever statements one hears one can comprehend all statements, all statements and all principles without hindrance.

It is difficult to understand the meaning of multiple understandings of one statement. It may be further explained in terms of the *Treatise on the Center.* When it says, "Phenomena produced by causal conditions I say are empty," since it says "produced by causal conditions," how can they be empty just like that? It is necessary to analyze the causal conditions thoroughly, and only then does one finally comprehend emptiness. "Ultimately empty" is here expressed as "are empty." As for "this is also called artificial description," that which is compounded is powerless and does not stand alone; it depends on many conditions for its existence. It is "artificial" because of depending on conditions; this is not the "artifice" of setting up provisional expedients. As for "It is also called the meaning of the Middle Way," being apart from annihilation and eternity is called the Middle Way; this is not the Middle Way of the Buddha-nature.

If you understand in this way, though all three phrases indicate emptiness, this still does not mean immediate identification with emptiness, much less immediate identification with the conditional or the Middle Way. This is the meaning of the four truths of birth and death.

If one understands that things produced by causal conditions are inherently empty, without needing to be broken down and annihilated, yet they cannot be immediately identified with the conditional and the Middle Way, even if they are taken to be the conditional and the Middle Way, all enter into emptiness. Why? Because all things are themselves empty, having no self. The conditional too is empty, being conditional setups; and the Middle Way too is empty, being apart from the two extremes of annihilation and eternity. Though the three statements are different, they all enter emptiness; but here they do not regress back to the analytic method of the two vehicles, nor do they progress to the separate or complete teachings. This is just the meaning of common emptiness, symbolized by three animals crossing a river.

Suppose one takes the statement that all things are empty, conditional, and in the middle as meaning the three are interconnected but each has difference. Taking all three as expressions of emptiness, things have no master, and therefore are empty; they are unreal definitions and therefore are empty; they have no extremes and therefore are empty. Taking all three as expressions of conditionality, they all have names and are therefore conditional. Taking all three as expressions of the Middle Way, they refer to the truth of the center, the potential of the center, and the reality of the center, and are therefore all the Middle Way. This interpretation gets the separate but not the complete.

Suppose one takes the statements that all things are empty, conditional, and in the middle as meaning that even though the three are one, while one they are three, without mutual interference. Taking all three as referring to emptiness, it is because there is no way to express or think of [the empty essence of things]. Taking all three as referring to conditionality, it is because all things just have names [and no absolute identities]. Taking all three as referring to the Middle Way, it is because [all things] are the form of reality. Emptiness is just used as a label; conditionality and the center are automatically included. If one realizes emptiness, then one realizes conditionality and the center as well. This also applies to the other [terms of conditionality and the center].

You should know that people give rise to various understandings and make various vows on hearing one doctrine; this is variously arousing the determination for enlightenment. This should be understood. As for arousing the determination for enlightenment by seeing various pure lands, groups, practices, things perishing, people suffering, or errors being committed, these can be understood along the lines I have just set forth, and so I will not go into further detail.

A great deal has been said up to this point; now I will wrap it up [in terms of] three kinds of stopping and seeing. However, the nature of reality is not even one thing; how could we think of it in terms of three or four? Now, when we are saying one, two, three, or four, we are saying that the nature of reality is the object of confusion, suffering and its cause are the source of confusion; in the source of confusion there are differences in degree of gravity, while there is identity and detachment in the object of confusion. Distinguishing in terms of internal and external, there are four kinds of suffering and its cause, and apprehending principle in terms of faculties and temperaments, there are differences of one, two, three, and four.

The delusions of dull people in the world in regard to reality are heavy, so their suffering and its cause are also heavy. The delusions of keen people about the world are light, so their suffering and its cause are also light. Outside the world, the lightness and heaviness of the keen and the dull are also thus.

The nature of reality is that which is to be understood, the Way and extinction refer to the understanding. In the understood, there is identification and detachment; in the understanding, there is the skillful and the unskillful. That which is understood by dull people in the world is detachment; their understanding is unskillful. That which is understood by keen people is identification; their understanding is skillful. The identification and detachment, skillfulness and unskillfulness of the keen and the dull beyond the world is also like this.

Why is this? As phenomena and principle are disparate, unawareness and confusion are also severe. It is like a father and son thinking each other strangers, becoming angry, and coming to blows, both severely upset. The anger represents the cause of suffering, the beating represents suffering. If one considers afflictions to be identical to the nature of reality, phenomena and principle are identical; cause and suffering are thus light. Those who are not really relatives think themselves father and son, with the result that anger and blows are slight. This is also the way it is with coarse and fine, branch and root, common and particular, universal and nonuniversal, difficult and easy.

It may be said that the stagnancy in suffering and its cause within the world is heavy, while the rising up and out beyond the world is light. It may be said that the delusions within the world are shallow, and the delusions beyond the world are deep. It may be said that within the world one follows the will of another, so it is unskillful, while beyond the world one follows one's own will, so it is skillful. It may be said that within the world there is subject and object, so it is coarse, while beyond the world there is no subject and object, so it is fine.

It may be said that the small path within the world culminates in the magic city, so it is fine, while the great path beyond the world culminates in the abode of treasure, so it is coarse.

It may be said that within the world is external defilement, so it is secondary, while beyond the world is identity of being, so it is basic. It may be said that inside the world is first, so it is basic, while beyond the world is subsequent, so it is secondary.

It may be said that inside the world the Small and Great Vehicles are together, so it is common, while beyond the world is only in the Great Vehicle, so it is separate. It may be said that inside the world is one-sided, so it is small, and shallow, so it is separate, while beyond the world is complete, so it is great, and without barriers, so it is common.

It may be said that within the world is short, so it is not universal, while beyond the world pervades the cosmos, so it is universal. It may be said that within the world is in all sages and saints in common, so it is universal, while beyond the world is only in those with the great objective, so it is not universal.

Some say that within the world are used the techniques of the two vehicles, so it is hard to stop, while beyond the world only unobstructed wisdom is relied upon, so it is easy to stop.

Now, if we were to sum up these various contrasting statements, they could easily be understood. If one construes shallow and deep, light and heavy, this is the sense of gradual contemplation. If one construes four truths of one reality without discriminating, this is the sense of complete contemplation. If one construes interchanging light and heavy, this is the sense of unfixed contemplation. All of these are aspects of the way of the Great Vehicle, so one should know them. If one sees the sense of this, one will know the three kinds: the gradual reveals what is right, the unfixed reveals what is right, and the complete and immediate reveals what is right.

QUESTION: Since there are four kinds of cause, why are there only two kinds of suffering as a result?

ANSWER: In terms of delusion according to understanding, there are four kinds of cause; in terms of understanding according to delusion, only two kinds of death are experienced as a result. For example, as in the case of the lesser vehicle, in terms of delusion according to understanding, there are delusions of view and thought in seeing the truths and meditating; in terms of understanding according to delusion, there is only the one individual birth and death.

QUESTION: Suffering and its cause are admittedly phenomena produced by conditions, but why are the Path and extinction so?

ANSWER: Suffering and its cause are that which is to be broken through, the Path and extinction are that which breaks through. The breaker gets its name from the broken, so both are condition-produced phenomena. Therefore the major scripture says, "By annihilating ignorance, it is possible to light the lamp of perfect enlightenment." This is also conditional relation.

QUESTION: The nature of reality is that which is misunderstood; why is it twofold, why is it fourfold?

ANSWER: The nature of reality is twofold in terms of the provisional and the true; it is fourfold in terms of faculties and affinities.

Next, let us show what is right in terms of the universal vows. Previously we considered the nature of reality, hearing the Teaching, and so forth, and the meanings are clear. For those who have not yet understood, we go on to speak in terms of the four universal vows.

In the four truths, "seeking above and teaching below" is mostly explained in terms of understanding; in the four universal vows, seeking above and teaching below is mostly explained in terms of aspiration.

In the four truths, seeking above and teaching below is explained in reference to all the Buddhas of past, present, and future; in the four universal vows, seeking above and teaching below is mostly explained in terms of the Buddhas of the future.

Also, in the four truths, seeking above and teaching below is mostly explained in terms of all the faculties; while in the four vows, seeking above and teaching below is explained solely in terms of the intellectual faculty.

Such distinctions are made to facilitate understanding; those who get the idea do not need them.

Now, the mind does not arise alone but in relation to objects. The intellective faculty is the cause, the data of phenomena is the condition, and the mind aroused is that which is produced. This faculty and data, subject and object, become, change, and pass away, suddenly arising, suddenly vanishing, again and again being born and passing away anew, not abiding moment to moment, like flashes of lightning, swift as a rapids.

The foam of form, the bubbles of sensation, the flames of perception, the boundaries of conditioned states, the illusions of consciousness, all the objective counterparts of awareness, including land, fields, house, family, property—all are gone in an instant. Momentarily there, suddenly they are gone. The whole world is impermanent; the whole world is just suffering.

When the physical elements come together, there is no place to escape. One should only focus the mind on discipline, concentration, and wisdom, to vertically break up delusion and horizontally cut through the sea of death, crossing over the stream of existence. Scripture says, "In the past, I did not see the four truths, just like you; that is why I went around in circles for a long time." The "burning house" is like this; how can you be addicted to indulgence and amusement?

For this reason, compassion inspires the four universal vows, to remove suffering and give happiness. Examples of this are when Shakyamuni saw worms being turned up by a plow and devoured by crows, and when Maitreya saw a precious pedestal being destroyed. Because of expressing the comprehension of the four truths, it is not in the nine bonds; because of producing four universal vows, it is not one simplex liberation; this is arousing the genuine aspiration for enlightenment, neither in bondage nor in liberation. Thus the meaning of revealing what is right is clear.

Next, just contemplate the momentary arising of the mind in the relationship of sense faculty and data. What is produced by subject and object is all void; in error one thinks mind arises. The arising has no intrinsic essence, no relative essence, no common essence, and no causeless essence. When it arises, it does not come from itself, from another, from both itself and another, or apart from these. When it departs, it does not go east, west, south, or north. This mind is not inside, outside, or in between. Also, it does not exist permanently by itself. There is just a name, "mind." This word does not abide, nor does it not abide.

Because it cannot be grasped, birth itself is birthless, and yet there is no birthlessness; existence and nonexistence are both null. The ordinary ignorant person thinks it exists, the sage knows it does not. It is like the moon reflected in water. The childish are joyful when they get something, sad when they lose it; but the mature get rid of grasping and are free from joy and sorrow. This is the way it is with reflections in a mirror, or magically produced illusions.

The *Scripture on Consideration of Benefit* says, "Suffering has no birth, accumulation, or compounding; the path is nondual, extinction is unborn." The *Great Perfect Nirvana Scripture* says, "Understand there is no suffering in suffering, yet there is truth. . . . Understand there is no extinction in extinction, yet there is truth." Since the cause of accumulating suffering is itself empty, one should not be like a thirsty deer chasing a mirage. Since suffering is itself empty, one should not be like a foolish monkey grasping at the moon in the water. Since the Path is itself empty, one should not say "I practice emptiness" or "I do not practice emptiness." It is like the metaphor of the raft—even the Teaching should be left behind, to say nothing of what is contrary to the Teaching. Since extinction is itself empty, one should not speak of sentient beings and life—who becomes extinct here and experiences that extinction? Since the cyclic routine of birth and death is empty, how is it to be abandoned? Since nirvana is empty, how is it to be attained?

Scripture says, "I do not wish to have there be practice of the Path—from the four points of mindfulness to the eightfold holy Path—in birthless reality; I do not wish to have there be attainment of fruits—from stream enterer to sainthood—in birthless reality." According to this example, it should say, "I do not wish to have there be form, sensation, perception, conformation, and consciousness in birthless reality; I do not wish to have there be greed, hatred, and delusion in birthless reality. But out of compassion for sentient beings, I vow to relieve suffering and give happiness." Because of realizing that suffering and the cause of its accumulation are empty, it is not one liberation; this is arousing the genuine aspiration for enlightenment that is neither bound nor liberated.

Just observe the momentary arising of mind in the relationship of the sense faculties and sense data; the arising of mind is conditional, and the mind of conditional terminology is the basis of delusion and understanding. This means the four truths have infinite characteristics; there is nothing else in the triple world but the making of one mind, and the mind is like a painter, making various forms. The mind constructs the six states of existence and discriminates and compares infinitely various differences, such as, for example, that such and such views and cravings are characteristic of light or heavy causes of suffering in the world or characteristic of light or heavy causes of suffering beyond the world, or that such and such birth and death is characteristic of light or heavy suffering of individual birth and death, or characteristic of light or heavy birth and death beyond the world. By overturning this mind, one produces understanding, like a painter washing off colors and applying whitewash.

That means contemplating the body as impure and mind as inconstant. These items of the path lead indirectly to the magic citadel.

Contemplating the body as empty, observing mind as empty, seeing no impermanence and no impurity in emptiness—such items of the path lead directly to the magic citadel.

When contemplating the body as impermanent, you see impermanence is identical to emptiness. Contemplating the reality nature of the body, you see it is not permanent, not impermanent, not empty, not nonempty. Contemplating the mind is also like this. Such items of the path lead indirectly to the abode of treasure.

Contemplating the real nature of the body as neither pure nor impure, yet aware of both purity and impurity, and so on, contemplating the real nature of the mind as neither permanent nor impermanent, yet aware of both permanence and impermanence, such items of the path lead directly to the abode of treasure.

For certain people, the extinction of delusions of views is called entering the stream. For some people, the extinction of delusions of thought is called the third stage of realization. For some people, the extinction of delusions of views is called the stage of insight. For some people, the extinction of delusions of thought is called lightness, detachment, or being finished; when thoroughly developed, it is called individual enlightenment.

For some people, extinction of delusions of views and thoughts is called the ten abodes; the extinction of the delusions as numerous as dust particles and sand grains is called the ten practices and ten dedications; and the extinction of the delusion of ignorance is called the ten stages, equivalency to enlightenment, and ineffable enlightenment. For some people, the extinction of delusions of views, delusions of thought, and the delusions as numerous as particles of dust and grains of sand is called the ten stages of faith, while the delusion of ignorance is called the ten abodes, ten practices, ten dedications, ten stages, equivalency to enlightenment, and ineffable enlightenment.

Distinguishing differences in the path and extinction in sixteen ways, and in all the innumerable Buddhist teachings distinguishing and comparing untold differences, without any bias or error, as clearly and plainly as looking at a fruit in the palm of one's hand, all comes from the mind, nowhere else. Observing this one mind, you can comprehend untold minds; untold minds can comprehend untold principles; untold principles can lead to the unspeakable that is neither mind nor principle. Observing all minds is also done in this way.

Ordinary people caught in bondage are unaware and do not know, like blind children of a rich family sitting in a storehouse of treasures without seeing any of them, just bumping into them when they move and thus being wounded by the treasures. Those of the two vehicles, in their fever, think the treasures are ghosts and tigers, dragons and snakes; they reject them and run away, wandering in misery for fifty-odd years. Although these two types differ in bondage and liberation, both lack the supreme treasure of the Buddhas, those who arrive at thusness. Producing a great compassionate vow to remove their pains and give them happiness is arousing the genuine aspiration for enlightenment, neither in bondage nor in liberation.

Next, the momentary arising of mind in the relation of sense and data is empty, is conditional, and is the Middle Way: whether sense faculties or sense data, all are the realm of reality, all are ultimately empty, all are the matrix of the realization of thusness, all are the Middle Way.

How are they empty? All are born of conditions, and what is of conditional origin has no independent basis, and what has no independent basis is empty.

How are they conditional? That which is born without independent basis is conditional.

How are they the Middle Way? Not apart from the nature of reality, all are the mean.

You should know a thought is empty, is conditional, is in the middle; all are ultimate emptiness, all are the matrix of realization of thusness, all are characteristic of reality. They are not three, yet are three; they are three, yet are not three. They neither combine nor dissolve, yet they do combine and do dissolve. They are not ununited, not indistinct; they cannot be considered one or different, they are one and they are different.

This may be likened to a clear mirror. The clarity is like emptiness, the images are like the conditional, the mirror is like the Middle Way. They are not united or disparate, but their unity and disparity are evident. They are not one, two, or three, yet are one, two, and three nevertheless.

This mental moment is not vertical, not horizontal; it is inconceivable. This is not true only of oneself; Buddhas and sentient beings are also thus. The *Flower Ornament Scripture* says, "Mind, Buddha, sentient beings—these three have no difference." You should know your own mind contains all Buddha's principles. The *Scripture on*

Consideration of Benefit says, "The ignorant want to seek enlightenment in the elements of mind and matter, but these elements are themselves it—apart from these there is no enlightenment." The *Pure Name Scripture* says, "The liberation of Buddhas is to be sought in the mental activities of sentient beings. Sentient beings *are* enlightenment, which cannot be further attained; sentient beings *are* nirvana, and cannot be further extinguished." As one mind is thus, so are all minds, and so are all things. When the *Contemplation of Universal Good* says that Vairochana Buddha is omnipresent, this is what it means. You should know that all things are teachings of Buddha, because the Buddha is the cosmos.

But if so, how then can it be said one roams in the mental cosmos, as if it were space? And it is also said that when ignorance is understood, it is ultimate emptiness. These say-ings speak from the basis of emptiness; emptiness is not empty, and it is also neither empty nor nonempty.

It is also said that a cosmic scripture is contained in an individual atom and that the mind contains all Buddhist principles, like the earth containing seeds or like a ball of fragrances. These sayings speak from the basis of exis-tence; existence is not existence, and it is also neither ex-istent nor nonexistent.

It is also said that each form, each scent, is the Middle Way. This speaks from the basis of the Middle Way; the Middle Way is itself the extremes, and is neither extreme nor not extreme. It is all there, nothing lacking—do not stick to words at the expense of completeness, miscon-struing the intent of the sage.

If you attain this understanding, in the momentary arising of mind in the relation of sense faculties and data, the sense faculties are the repository of the eighty-four thousand teachings, and so are the data. The moment of arising of mind is also the repository of the eighty-four thousand teachings. The definitions of truths arising from the realm of Buddhist principles relative to the realm of phenomena are all enlightened teachings.

The identity of the birth-death cycle and nirvana is called the truth of suffering. Each sense datum is trifold, each mental state is trifold. Each datum has eighty-four thousand doors of affliction, and so does each mental state. Greed, anger, and folly, too, are none other than enlightenment, and afflictions are enlightenment; this is called the truth of causality. Overturning each door of affliction is the eighty-four thousand doors of concentration, and it is also the eighty-four thousand doors of specific cures, and it also accomplishes the eighty-four thousand ways of transcendence.

When ignorance is overturned, it transmutes into enlightenment. It is like melting ice into water; it is not something apart and does not come from elsewhere. All is contained in a single moment of mind. It is like a wish-fulfilling jewel; it is not that it has treasures, nor does it not have treasures. If you say there is not, this is false; if you say there is, this is an erroneous view. It cannot be known by mind, cannot be explained in words.

People conceive of bondage in this nonbinding inconceivable reality and seek liberation in this reality where there is no liberation. Therefore we arouse great compassion and make the four universal vows, to remove their suffering and give them happiness. Therefore it is called arousal of the genuine aspiration for enlightenment, neither in bondage nor in liberation.

The first three are expressed in terms of the four truths, this one in terms of the repository of teachings, the afflictions, the concentrations, and the ways of transcendence.

QUESTION: Previously, when weeding out that which is wrong, it was all called wrong; now, in showing what is right, with what reason in each case is it called right?

ANSWER: It is in each case called right because it is neither bondage nor liberation, because in every case it is higher seeking. We also say they are all right because of progressive entry into truth. Also, the truth being difficult to know, using temporary expedients to reveal truth is called right in each case. These three are called right in reference to the aim of the world.

Also, temporary expedients do not contain the true; it is the true that contains temporary expedients. In order to make containing and revealing easy to see, we say they are all right. This case is said to be right in reference to the aim of helping people.

Also, one aspiration for enlightenment is all aspirations for enlightenment, but without explanation all are not known, so we say they are all right. In this case we explain right in terms of the aim of specific cure.

Speaking ultimately, the first three are in terms of temporary expedients, the last one in terms of the true. It is as if a physician had a secret prescription that included all prescriptions, a health-giving medicine whose effects included those of all medicines. It is like when you eat grain cooked in milk you do not need anything more. All is included, like in a wish-fulfilling jewel. The sense of expedient and true revealing what is right should be known.

Also, one "right" is in the sense of the cause and conditions of one great matter. How is it one? In terms of one truth not being false, one path being pure, all unimpeded people leaving the cycle of birth and death on one path. How is it great? Its nature is vast and inclusive; it is ridden by great people of great knowledge and great resolution; and the great lion roar greatly benefits the ordinary and the sage. Therefore it is called great. This "matter" is the procedure of the Buddhas of past, present, and future; by this they attain enlightenment, by this they liberate sentient beings. As for "cause and conditions," sentient beings sense Buddha by this cause, Buddha produces response by these conditions.

Also, in reference to "right," it cannot be called three, it cannot be called one, it cannot be called neither three nor one yet three and one; therefore it is called the inconceivable "right."

Again, in reference to "right," it is not a fabricated thing, not made by Buddha, by celestial beings, by humans, or by titans; the eternal sphere is signless, the eternal knowledge is objectless; with objectless knowledge perceiving the signless sphere, the signless sphere characterizing objectless knowledge, knowledge and sphere merge into one, yet are called sphere and knowledge. Therefore it is called uncreate.

Also, in reference to "right," the *Scripture of the Questions of Manjushri* says that breaking through everything is called arousing the aspiration for enlightenment; always following the characteristics of enlightenment, one arouses the aspiration for enlightenment. Also, it is arousing without arousing, following without following. Also, going beyond all breakthroughs, going beyond all following, yet simultaneously being aware of both breakthrough and following, is called arousing the aspiration for enlightenment. These three kinds are not one, not different, conforming to noumenon, conforming to phenomena, and according to neither noumenon nor phenomena; therefore this is called right.

In this sense, the teachings such as uncreate, inconceivable, the cause and conditions of the one great matter, and so on, all speak of breaking through, all speak of following, all speak of neither breakthrough nor following, simultaneously illuminating breakthrough and following.

Also, the first three are what is contemplated by those of superior, middling, and lesser knowledge; the last one is what is contemplated by most supreme knowledge. The first three, furthermore, are common, the last one is unique. The first three are shallow, nearby, and roundabout; the last one is deep, far, and direct. The first three are the great within the small; the last one is the great within the great, the best within the best, the complete within the complete, the full within the full, the true within the true, the real within the real, the comprehensive within the comprehensive, the mysterious within the mysterious, the marvelous within the marvelous, the inconceivable within the inconceivable.

If you can weed out what is wrong and reveal what is right in this way, comprehend the temporary and know the true, and thus arouse the inspiration, this is the seed of all Buddhas.

Just as iron comes from the nature of metal, the enlightenment inspiration of Buddhas comes from compassion. This is the forerunner of practices, just as one first drinks pure water before taking medicine; this is the foremost of practices, just as the faculty of life is the foremost of faculties.

In the right practice of the right teaching of Buddha, this aspiration for enlightenment is foremost, just as when a prince is born he has the marks of kingship, the ministers honor him, and he has a great name, and just as the voice of the kalavinka bird, even in the shell, is already superior to that of other birds, the aspiration for enlightenment has great power, like the sinews of a lion, like the milk of a lion, like an adamantine mallet, like the arrow of a hero. It is replete with many treasures and can eliminate the misery of poverty, like a wish-fulfilling jewel. Even though one with the aspiration for enlightenment may slack off a bit or be a bit remiss, one still surpasses the virtues of those of the two vehicles [who seek only personal liberation].

In sum, this aspiration contains all the virtues of enlightening beings and develops those who are supremely and truly awake, past, present, and future. If you understand this aspiration, you will naturally arrive at stopping and seeing. The nonexistence of arousal or obstruction is seeing, the quiescence of the essence is stopping. Stopping and seeing is enlightenment, enlightenment is stopping and seeing.

The *Scripture of the Jewel Bridge* says that if a mendicant does not cultivate the practice of mendicants, he does not even have a place to spit in all the universe; much less is he worthy of receiving offerings from people.

Sixty mendicants, weeping sadly, said to the Buddha,

"Even dying we cannot accept the offerings of others." The Buddha praised them for being repentant.

One mendicant said to Buddha, "What kind of mendicants can accept offerings?"

The Buddha said, "Those in this community who cultivate the practices of the community and gain the benefits of the community can accept offerings. Those in the four stages of progress and four stages of realization are members of this community. The thirty-seven elements of the Path are the practices of the community. The four realizations are the benefits of the community."

The mendicant asked, "What about those who develop the aspiration of the Great Vehicle?"

The Buddha said, "Those who arouse the aspiration of the Great Vehicle can accept offerings without membership, without practice, without realization."

The mendicant was surprised and asked how such people could accept offerings. The Buddha said, "Even if these people received cloth sufficient to cover the earth and mounds of rice as big as a mountain, they could still requite the benevolence of the donors."

So we should know that the ultimate fruit of the lesser vehicle does not equal the beginning aspiration of the Great Vehicle.

Also, the *Scripture on the Hidden Treasury of the Enlightened* says, "If one's father is an individual illuminate and one kills him or one steals what belongs to the Three Treasures, or one's mother is a saint and one defiles her or one falsely slanders a Buddha or one separates sages by duplicitous talk or one reviles sages with foul talk or one interferes with seekers of truth or one becomes so hostile as to commit heinous crimes or one becomes so greedy as to usurp the property of ethical people or one is so deluded as to embrace extreme views, these are the ten worst evils. But if one knows that conditioned phenomena, as explained by Buddha, have no self or person or soul or life, no birth, no destruction, no defilement, no detachment, and are essentially pure, and if knowing the essential purity of all phenomena one understands it and enters into it sincerely, I do not say this person will go to hell or wind up in other miserable states. Why? Phenomena have no accumulation, no accumulation of affliction; nothing is born, nothing remains. Because of the coalescence of conditions, they come to exist, but then they pass away. If the mind passes away after arising, all bondage and compulsion also pass away after arising. In this way one understands there is no transgression; there can be no transgression, no remaining. It is like when you light a lamp in a dark room: the darkness cannot claim rights over the room and cannot refuse to go just because it has been there for a long time. As soon as the lamp is lit, the darkness vanishes."

This scripture points to all of the aforementioned aspirations for enlightenment. "If one knows conditional phenomena as explained by Buddha" points to the first aspiration for enlightenment. "No birth, no destruction" points to the second aspiration for enlightenment. "Essentially pure" points to the third aspiration for enlightenment. "If one knows the essential purity in all things" points to the fourth aspiration for enlightenment. The first aspiration for enlightenment can already get rid of the most serious ten evils; how much more so can the second, third, and fourth aspirations for enlightenment!

When practitioners hear of this excellent virtue, they should be glad, as if they had found light and fragrance where there had been darkness and foulness.

QUESTION: In reference to clarifying what is right in terms of the six identities, is the beginning state of mind it, or is the final state of mind it?

ANSWER: It is like talking about burning a candle: it is not beginning, yet not apart from beginning, not final, yet not apart from ending. If knowledge and faith are complete, when one hears that a single instant is *it*, by virtue of faith one does not repudiate it, and by virtue of knowledge one does not fear it. Beginning and end are both right, both *it*.

If one has no faith, one will elevate it to the sphere of sages and think one has no knowledge of it. If one has no knowledge, one will become conceited and think one is equal to Buddha. Then beginning and end are both wrong, both not it.

Because of this, one should know the six identities: identity in principle, identity in words, identity in contemplative practices, identity in conformity, identity in partial realization, and ultimate identity. Beginning in the ordinary, they get rid of doubt and cowardice; ending in the holy, they get rid of conceit and arrogance.

As for noumenal identity, the mind in an instant of awareness is identical to the noumenon of the matrix of realization of thusness. Being "thus," it is identical to emptiness; being a "matrix," it is identical to the conditional; being "noumenon," it is identical to the mean.

The three knowledges are present in one mind, inconceivable, as previously explained. Three truths and one truth are not three, not one. Each datum of sense includes all phenomena. The same is true of all states of mind. This is called the noumenal identity; this is the mind of enlightenment. This is also noumenal stopping and seeing: being tranquil is called stopping, being aware is called seeing.

As for identity in words, though the noumenon is used every day, people don't know it. Because they have not heard of the three truths, they are ignorant of Buddhism, like oxen and sheep who cannot tell direction. When they have heard of the one true enlightenment as expounded above, whether from a teacher or from a scripture, and they understand the words and know all phenomena are Buddhist teachings, this is called words identical to enlightenment. This is also stopping and seeing of words. Before one has heard, one chases all over in search, but once one has heard, the clinging, searching mind stops; this is called stopping. Just trusting in the nature of reality and not in so many names is called seeing.

As for identity in contemplative practice, if one just hears words and only talks about them, this is like insects chewing wood happening to form the pattern of words; the insects do not know if they are words or not. Without realization, how can it be enlightenment? It is necessary that mind be clear, that principle and intellect be in harmony, that what is practiced be in accord with what is said, and what is said be in accord with what is practiced. The *Handfuls of Flowers Scripture* says, "Many do not practice what they talk about; I do not use talk, I just mentally practice enlightenment." This is correspondence of mind and speech. This is the enlightenment of contemplative practice.

In the *Great Treatise on Transcendent Wisdom* it speaks of four relations of learning and intelligence. Intelligence without learning is like having eyes in the dark. Learning without intelligence is like having a lamp in the daytime. Having neither learning nor intelligence is like being an ox with a human body. Having both learning and intelligence is like having eyes in the daylight, clearly perceiving without error. Contemplative practice is also like this; even when it has not harmonized with the noumenon, if the contemplating mind does not stop, it is like practicing archery, gradually learning to hit the target. This is called the enlightenment of contemplative practice, and it is also called the stopping and seeing of contemplative practice. Constantly performing this contemplation is called seeing; the cessation of other thoughts is called stopping.

As for conformity being identical to enlightenment, the more one sees, the clearer one becomes, and the more one stops, the calmer one becomes; it is like practicing shooting, getting nearer and nearer to the target. This is called conformative contemplative wisdom. All worldly livelihood and productive work is not opposed to it, all thoughts and judgments have been explained in the scriptures of the past Buddhas. As explained in the purification of the six senses, completely subduing ignorance is called stopping, knowledge in conformity with the Middle Way is called seeing.

As for partial realization, by the power of conformative contemplation one enters the rank of the bronze wheel sovereign. Breaking through ignorance and seeing Buddha-nature for the first time, opening up the jewel treasury and revealing true thusness, this is called the station of inspiration; ignorance becomes slighter and wisdom becomes progressively more pronounced, until equivalent enlightenment is reached. It is like the moonlight increasing toward fullness from the first to the fourteenth day of the lunar month, the darkness approaching the vanishing point. If people are to be liberated by the embodiment of a Buddha, one then fulfills the Way in eight forms; for those who are to be liberated by embodiments of the other nine realms of being, one manifests them by the medium of universality, as extensively explained in the *Lotus Scripture*. This is called the enlightenment of partial realization, and it is also called the stopping and seeing of partial realization, the knowledge and annihilation of partial realization.

As for ultimate identity with enlightenment, it is one step from equivalent enlightenment into ineffable enlightenment. The light of knowledge is complete and cannot be further increased; this is called the fruition of enlightenment. Great nirvana annihilates so that there is nothing more that can be annihilated; this is called the fruition of fruition. Equivalent enlightenment cannot comprehend it; only a Buddha can comprehend it. Beyond omega, there is no way to explain; therefore it is called ultimate enlightenment, and it is also called ultimate stopping and seeing.

To sum it all up with a simile, it is like a poor family with a treasure in their house that they do not know about; when one who knows points it out to them, then they know about it. Cleaning away the weeds and trash and excavating, they gradually get closer and closer to it.

After having come upon it, when the treasury is opened up, they can take from it and use the treasure.

QUESTION: What is the meaning of fivefold enlightenment in the treatise on wisdom?

ANSWER: The treatise vertically analyzes the separate stage; here we are vertically analyzing the complete stage. To reconcile them, "inspiration" corresponds to "words," "subduing the mind" corresponds to "contemplative practice," "clarifying the mind" corresponds to "conformity," "going forth and arriving" corresponds to "partial realization," and "unexcelled" corresponds to "ultimate."

Also, using these terms to label the stages of the complete teaching, "inspiration" is the ten abodes, "subduing the mind" is the ten practices.

QUESTION: In the ten abodes there is already cutting off; how can the practices be "subduing"?

ANSWER: This is using the real path to subdue. It is like the Way breaking through views is called "cutting off" in the Small Vehicle, while breaking through thought is called "subduing."

[To continue,] "clarifying the mind" is the ten dedications, "going forth and arriving" is the ten stages, and "unexcelled" is ineffable enlightenment.

There is also fivefold enlightenment from the ten abodes onward; when one gets to ineffable enlightenment, one consummates the fivefold enlightenment.

Therefore the *Treatise on the Ten Stages* says that one has the virtues of all the stages from the very first stage. This is the same meaning.

QUESTION: What is the meaning of speaking of the six identities in terms of the complete teaching?

ANSWER: Completely seeing all the teachings, which all bespeak the six identities, with the meaning of the complete teaching, we therefore use the six identities to define stages when dealing with all the teachings. This is not so of those teachings other than the complete teaching, so we do not use them, but how could it be inappropriate to apply the six identities to those teachings? The shallow and obvious is not the true meaning of the teachings.

So in the foregoing we have weeded out the incorrect. First we just did so in terms of the truth of suffering, the ups and downs in the world. Next we just did so in terms of the knowledge of the four truths, which is roundabout and clumsy, shallow and obvious. Next we used the four universal practical vows, then the stages of the six identities, progressively getting deeper and finer, finally revealing what is right.

So we know the spiritual pearl of the bright moon lies under the black dragon's jaw at the bottom of the ninefold abyss; only those with will and virtue can reach it. It is not like worldly people, coarse and shallow, unstable and vacuous, who compete to grasp shards and pebbles, straw and wood, and deludedly consider them jewels, having studied little and absorbed less, extremely ignorant.

II

THE SECOND ISSUE IS EXPLAINING THIS
stopping and seeing so as to promote four kinds of concentration by which to enter the ranks of enlightening beings. One cannot ascend to the sublime states without
practice; if you know how to churn, only then can you ob-
tain ghee.

The *Lotus Scripture* says, "Aspirants to Buddhahood
cultivate various practices, seeking enlightenment." There
are many methods of practice, but in general we speak of
four: constant sitting, constant walking, half walking and
half sitting, and neither walking nor sitting. The general
term *concentration* means tuning, aligning, and stabilizing.

The *Great Treatise* says, "Ability to keep the mind on
one point without wavering is called concentration." The
realm of reality is one point; correct seeing can stay on it
without wavering. The four practices are cooperating
conditions, by which the contemplating mind is tuned
and aligned; therefore they are called concentrations.

The first mode, constant sitting, comes from the two
sutras on transcendent wisdom called *Manjushri Speaks*

and *The Questions of Manjushri*. First I will explain the method, then explain how to promote its practice. Regarding method, in reference to the body the issue is what is permitted and what is forbidden; in reference to speech the issue is talk and silence; in reference to mind the issue is stopping and seeing.

Physically, sitting is what is permitted; walking, standing, and reclining are stopped. One may be in a community, but being alone is better. One stays in a quiet room or a deserted place, apart from all clamor. Only one seat is set up, with none beside it. The period of practice is ninety days. One sits crosslegged, with the neck and back straight, not moving, not wavering, not slouching, not leaning. Sitting, one vows one's sides will not touch a bed, much less lie like a corpse or fool around. Aside from meditative circumambulation, meals, and answering the calls of nature, one sits straight facing the direction of one Buddha, continuously, without a break. That which is permitted is only sitting; do not do what is prohibited and you will not cheat Buddha, betray the mind, or fool other people.

As for speech and silence, if one is thoroughly exhausted from sitting, or overcome by sickness, or enshrouded in sleepiness, invaded by inner and outer obstacles that take away correct mindfulness and cannot be removed, then one should chant the name of one Buddha, repenting and taking refuge in the Buddha. The virtue of this is equal to that of chanting the names of the Buddhas of the ten directions. Why? It is like when people are sad or happy or depressed, they sing or cry or lament or laugh, and then they feel better. So it is with the practitioner; the action of the breath and voice are physical and verbal action, which serve to help the mind and develop the organism, to feel the immanence of Buddha. It is like when someone is pulling a heavy load and cannot make progress on his own strength; he gets help from others, so that the weight is easily lifted. So it is with the practitioner; when the mind is feeble and cannot get rid of obstacles, if you chant a Buddha name seeking protection, bad conditions cannot harm you. If you have not yet comprehended the teachings, you should associate with those who understand wisdom, and practice what you learn from them, then you can enter into absorption in one practice, see the Buddhas face to face, and ascend to the stages of enlightening beings. Even reciting scriptures and spells disturbs quietude; how much the more does worldly talk!

As for the stopping and seeing of the mind, sitting straight, correctly mindful, one clears away wrong consciousness and abandons errant thoughts. Do not think at random, or grab on to appearances; just focus solely on the realm of reality. With one thought on the realm of reality, focusing is stopping, and one thought is seeing. When you believe all phenomena are the teaching of Buddha, there is no before or after; there are no more boundaries. There is no knower, no speaker. If there is no knowing or speaking, it is not existent or nonexistent. One is neither knower nor nonknower; apart from these extremes, one abides where there is nothing to dwell on, just as the Buddhas abide, resting in the silent realm of reality. Do not be afraid of this profound teaching.

This realm of reality is also called enlightenment, and it is also called the inconceivable realm. It is also called wisdom, and it is also called not being born and not passing away. Thus all phenomena are not other than the realm of reality; hearing of this nonduality and nondifference, do not give rise to doubt.

If you can see in this way, this is seeing the ten epithets of Buddhas. When seeing Buddha, one does not consider Buddha as Buddha; there is no Buddha to be Buddha, and there is no Buddha-knowledge to know Buddha. Buddha and Buddha-knowledge are nondualistic, unmoving, unfabricated, not in any location yet not unlocated, not in time yet not timeless, not dual yet not nondual, not defiled, not pure. This seeing Buddha is very rarefied; like space, it has no flaw, and it develops right mindfulness.

Seeing the embellishments of Buddha is like looking into a mirror and seeing one's own features. First you see one Buddha, then the Buddhas of the ten directions. You do not use magical powers to go see Buddhas; you stay right here and see the Buddhas, hear the Buddhas' teaching, and get the true meaning. You see the Buddha for all beings, yet do not grasp the form of Buddha. You guide all beings toward nirvana, yet do not grasp the characteristics of nirvana. You produce great adornments for all beings, yet do not grasp the forms of adornment. No form, no sign, no seeing, no cognition, Buddha does not witness; this is considered wonderful. Why? Buddha is identical to the realm of reality; for the realm of reality to witness the realm of reality would be a contradiction. There is no witness, no attainment. You see the appearances of beings as like the appearances of Buddhas, and you see the extent of the realm of beings as like the extent of the realm of Buddhas. The extent of the realm of Buddhas is inconceivable; the extent of the realm of sentient beings is also inconceivable. The abode of the realm of sentient beings is like the abode of space.

By the principle of nondwelling, by the principle of signlessness, abiding in transcendent wisdom, you do not see anything profane; what is there to abandon? You do not see anything holy; what is there to grasp? So it is also of samsara and nirvana, defilement and purity; not rejecting, not grasping, you just abide in reality.

In this way, you see living beings as the true reality realm of Buddha. You see desire, anger, folly, and other afflictions as ever tranquil action. This is immutable practice, neither samsaric nor nirvanic, practicing the Buddha Way without abandoning views, without abandoning the uncreate. It is not practicing the Way, yet not not practicing the Way. This is called correct abiding in the reality realm of afflictions.

As for seeing the weight of acts, none is more serious than the five sins, yet the five sins are none other than enlightenment; the five sins and enlightenment are nondual. There is no cognizer, no knower, no discriminator; the appearance of sins and the appearance of reality are both inconceivable and indestructible. Basically there is no fundamental essence. All conditions of action abide at the limit of reality, not coming or going, neither cause nor effect. This is called seeing action as identical to the impression of the reality realm. The impression of the reality realm cannot be destroyed or affected by the four demons. Why? Demons are none other than the impression of the reality realm; how can the impression of the reality realm destroy the impression of the reality realm? All things can be understood in this way.

The foregoing exposition is scriptural. As for promoting practice, extolling the true virtues and encouraging practitioners, the teaching of the reality realm is the real teaching of Buddha, the seal of bodhisattvas; if you hear this teaching and are not startled or frightened, that means you have long planted roots of virtue with millions of Buddhas. Just as a rich man who has lost a jewel is very joyful upon finding it, as long as people do not hear this teaching their minds are pained and afflicted; but if they hear it, believe and understand it, and rejoice in accord, know that such people see Buddha and have already heard this teaching from Manjushri.

Shariputra said, "One who clearly understands this doctrine is called a bodhisattva, or enlightening being, a mahasattva, or great being." Maitreya said, "Such a person approaches the seat of Buddha, because Buddha is aware of this truth." Manjushri said, "To hear this teaching without being upset is itself seeing Buddha." Buddha said, "Then one abides in the stage of nonregression, replete with the six perfections, replete with all qualities of Buddhahood." If you want to attain all qualities of Buddhahood, the marks and refinements of greatness, the dignity of bearing, the voice of teaching truth, the ten powers, and the fearlessnesses, you should carry out this one-practice concentration. If you practice diligently, you will be able to enter into it. It is like polishing a jewel; the more you polish, the more it shines. Realizing inconceivable virtues, bodhisattvas can know they will soon attain enlightenment; for monks and nuns to hear of it without alarm is to leave home to follow Buddha; for believing men and women to hear of it without alarm is to truly take refuge. This way of extolling the practice comes from the aforementioned two scriptures.

The second practice is constant walking concentration. First I will explain the method, then promote the practice. Method involves what is allowed and not allowed, for the body; speech and silence; and stopping and seeing, for the mind. This method comes from the *Pratyutpannasamadhi-sutra*, which is translated in Chinese as "The Scripture on Buddha Standing Concentration." "Buddha standing" has three meanings: the spiritual power of Buddha, the power of concentration, and the power of basic virtues of the practice. By these, you can, in concentration, see the present Buddhas of the ten directions standing before you. Just like when someone with keen eyes sees stars on a clear night, when you see the Buddhas of the ten directions, there are very many. Thus it is called Buddha standing concentration.

A verse of a commentary on the ten stages says, "In the abode of concentration there are distinctions of little, medium, and much; these various characteristics should also be discussed." As for "abode," in the first, second, third, or fourth stages of meditation, one may release this power and be able to produce the concentration, so it is referred to by the term *abode*. The first stage of meditation is "little," the second is "medium," the third and fourth are "much." Alternatively, abiding for a little time may be called little, or it may be called little because one sees few worlds or few Buddhas. This also applies to "medium" and "much."

In terms of the body, what is permitted in this concentration exercise is constant walking. When practicing this method, you should avoid bad associates, ignoramuses, relatives, and acquaintances. You should always remain alone and not look for other people or seek for any thing.

You should beg for your food and not accept special invitations. Adorning the place of practice, providing ceremonial offerings, fragrant food and sweet fruit, you wash your body and change your clothes regularly.

The period of practice is ninety days, during which you only walk around. You need an illumined teacher who is expert in inner and outer discipline and is able to remove obstacles. In the concentration you learn from the teacher, you look upon the teacher as upon Buddha, without aversion or anger, not seeing weaknesses or strengths. You would even tear off your skin and flesh to offer the teacher, to say nothing of other things. You serve the teacher like a servant working for an employer. If you dislike the teacher, it will be hard to get into this concentration. You need outside supporters, like a mother taking care of a child, and you need fellow practitioners, as if you were all walking a dangerous road together. You should vow to learn this concentration even if your sinews and bones wither and rot. You should not stop or rest. Arouse great faith that none can destroy, arouse great energy that none can equal, enter great knowledge that none can reach.

Always attending a good teacher, throughout the three months do not think of worldly imaginations and desires for even a moment. Walking should not stop throughout the three months, except to sit for meals, answer the calls of nature, and wash. When explaining scriptures to others, you should not hope to be given food or clothing. A verse of the previously quoted commentary says, "Associate with a benefactor, vigor unflagging, wisdom most firm, the power of the Path immovable."

As for speech and silence, as the body constantly walks without cease for ninety days, the mouth constantly chants the name of Amitabha Buddha for ninety days, and the mind constantly thinks of Amitabha Buddha for ninety days. The chanting and thinking may go on to-gether, or one may think first and then chant, or chant first and then think. Chanting and thinking continue without stop. If you chant the name of Amitabha, the Buddha of Infinite Light, the virtue is the same as chant-ing the names of the Buddhas of the ten directions. Just consider Amitabha the focus of the teaching. In sum, each step, each utterance, each thought, is solely on Amitabha Buddha.

As for stopping and seeing in the mind, think of Amitabha Buddha in the West, ten trillion buddha-lands from here, in a jewel temple on a jewel ground with jewel ponds and jewel trees, sitting in the middle of enlighten-ing be-ings, speaking scripture. For three months, always think of Buddha.

How do you think of Buddha? Think of the thirty-two marks of greatness; from the thousand-spoked wheels on the soles of the feet, think of the marks one after another up to the invisible crown. Then go from the invisible crown down to the thousand-spoked wheels, with the thought that you may be enabled to attain these marks.

Also think in this way: "Would I attain Buddhahood from the mind or from the body? Buddhahood is not at-tained by means of mind or body. The form of Buddha is not attained by means of mind, the mind of Buddha is not attained by means of form. Why? As for mind, Buddha has no mind; as for form, Buddha has no form. Therefore perfect enlightenment is not attained by means of matter or mind. The physical form, sensation, conception, mental formations, and consciousness of Buddha are already extinct. The extinction spoken of in reference to Buddha is unknown to the ignorant but understood by the wise. One does not attain Buddhahood by body or speech, or by intellect. Why? When you look for the intellect, it cannot be grasped; when you search for your self, it cannot be grasped. Also, nothing is seen. All things fundamentally have no existence and are totally void of even this fundamental nonexistence."

Seeing treasures or relatives in a dream, you are happy; when you think of them upon awakening, you do not know where they are. Think of Buddha in this way. Also, suppose there is a girl whose very name delights the heart, and at night one dreams of making love with her; after awakening, thinking of her, though she has not come to you and you have not gone to her, yet the pleasures were manifest. Think of Buddha in this way. Someone traveling in a wasteland, hungry and thirsty, dreams of getting fine food, then finds his belly empty upon awakening, and reflects that all things are like dreams. Think of Buddha in this way. Reflecting over and over again, do not stop. By this reflection you should be born in the land of Amitabha Buddha. This is called thinking of Buddha in terms of similitudes. It is like someone putting a jewel on crystal, so reflections appear therein. It is also like a monk contemplating bones, with the bones producing various kinds of light. No one brings the reflection, and there are no such bones; they are mentally produced, that is all. Reflections in a mirror do not come from outside and do not arise within; one spontaneously sees one's features because the mirror is clear. Insofar as the practitioner is physically pure, what is there is pure: wishing to see Buddha, you see Buddha; seeing Buddha, you ask questions, and the questions are answered. Hearing this discourse, you are very joyful.

Think to yourself, "Where does Buddha come from? And I go nowhere. I see what I think of; mind makes Buddha, mind itself seeing mind sees the Buddha mind. This Buddha mind is my mind seeing Buddha. Mind does not itself know mind, mind does not itself see mind. When there are thoughts in the mind, this is confusion; when there are no thoughts in the mind, this is nirvana. There is no representing this teaching; all is made by thought. Even if there is thought, still ultimately there is nothing, it being empty."

Consider the following verses:

> *Mind does not know mind;*
> *having a mind, one does not see mind.*
> *Producing thoughts is confusion;*
> *no thought is nirvana.*

> *The Buddhas attain liberation by way of mind;*
> *the mind, without defilement, is called pure:*
> *immaculate in all states of being, it does not take*
>   *on form.*
> *Those who understand this attain the great Way.*

This is called the Buddha-seal. There is nothing to crave, nothing to seek, nothing to think. All that exists is ended, all that is desired is ended. Nothing is born from it, nothing can perish. Nothing is destroyed. This is the essence of the Path, the basis of the Path. This seal cannot be broken by the two vehicles of individual salvation, much less by demons or hypocrites.

Commentary explains that a newly inspired enlightening being first meditates on the characteristics of the physical form of Buddha, the essence of the characteristics, the actions of the characteristics, the fruits of the characteristics, and the function of the characteristics, and thus attains lower power. Then one meditates on the unique qualities of Buddhas, and the mind attains middling power. Then one meditates on the real Buddha and gains superior power. Yet one does not cling to two bodies, physical and spiritual; a verse says, "Not attached to the physical body or to the spiritual body, one knows all things are eternally quiescent, like space."

As for promoting practice, if people want to attain oceanic wisdom such that no one can be their teacher, and see the Buddhas right here without using occult powers, hear their teachings and be able to absorb and retain them all, constant walking concentration is most efficacious. This concentration is the mother of the Buddhas: the enlightened eye is the father of Buddhas, uncreated universal compassion is the mother; all the Buddhas are born from these two things.

If all the land and vegetation of a universe were reduced to atoms, and each atom were a Buddha-land, and you filled that many worlds with jewels and used them for offerings, the merit in that would be very much, but not as much as hearing of this concentration without alarm or fear; there is even more merit in believing in it, absorbing and retaining it, reading about it, and explaining it to others, even more in practicing it with a focused mind even for a while, even more in being able to accomplish the concentration, in which there is measureless merit.

Commentary says it is impossible for the eonic fire, government officials, robbers, enemies, vipers, beasts, or sickness to attack such people; such people are always protected and praised by celestial beings and Buddhas, and all come to see them. If you hear of these four levels of merit and rejoice, the Buddhas and bodhisattvas of all times all rejoice; this surpasses even those four levels of merit. If you do not practice this teaching, you lose a treasure of measureless value, and human and celestial beings will grieve over this. You will be like one whose nose is cut off, who has sandalwood but cannot smell it; like a bumpkin who trades a jewel for an ox.

The third mode of concentration is half walking and half sitting. Again, I will first explain the method, then promote the practice. Method involves what to do and what not to do, speech and silence, stopping and seeing. This comes from two scriptures. A *Universally Equal* scripture says, "Circumambulate one hundred and twenty times, then sit and meditate." The *Lotus Scripture* says, "If people recite this scripture while walking or standing, or sit and contemplate this scripture, I will appear before them riding on a six-tusked white elephant." So we know half walking and half sitting is the mode; the *Universally Equal* scripture is most honorable, not to be slighted.

If you want to practice this, the spiritual luminaries are witnesses. First seek the dream kings; if you get to see one, that means your repentance is accepted. Arrange a practice site in a quiet place; paint the ground and inside and outside the room with fragrant paste, set up a round altar and paint it, hang pennants of five colors, burn sandalwood incense, light lamps, and set up a high seat. Set up twenty-four icons or more, and set out offerings of food, using your utmost attention. You should wear new clothing and footwear; if you have no new ones, clean old ones. Do not let them get mixed up as you put them on and take them off when going in and out. For seven days do not eat after noon, and bathe three times a day.

On the first day, present offerings to mendicants, as much or as little as wished. Ask one who clearly understands the inner and outer disciplines to be the guide. Receive the precepts and the mystic spells, and tell the teacher of your faults. The eighth to the fifteenth day of the month should be used. The period of practice is seven days; it should definitely not be shortened. If you can go on longer, you may do so as you wish. The number of participants should be no more than ten; lay people may participate, but they should dress according to the Buddhist rites.

As for speech and silence, first recite a spell until you can do it fluently. In the mornings everyone chants in unison. Three times, summon and entreat the Three Treasures, Ten Buddhas, Provisional and True Knowledge, and Ten Bodhisattvas. [The way of doing this is in *A Hundred Records of Clarification for the Nation*.] When the entreaty is ended, mindfully offer up your body, speech, and mind as you kneel, chant, and meditate. When the offering is finished, bow to the Three Treasures. When the bowing is finished, confess and repent of your faults and misdeeds, weeping with determination and sincerity. After this, rise and circumambulate one hundred and twenty times, uttering one spell each time, neither slowly nor quickly, neither loudly nor softly. After circumambulation and incantation, bow to the ten Buddhas, the *Universally Equal* scriptures, and the ten bodhisattvas. Having done this, sit and meditate. After meditating, get up again, circle and chant. When finished circling and chanting, sit down again and meditate. Repeat this cycle over and over for seven days. This is the method. From the second time on, the summons and entreaty are omitted, but the rest is the same.

As for mental stopping and seeing, scripture calls for meditation on a spell known as "the great mystic essential preventing evil and maintaining good." The "mystic essential" is just reality, the Middle Way, true emptiness. The scripture says, "I come from reality. Reality is quiescent. In quiescence, there is nothing sought, and the seeker too is empty. The attainer, the clinger, the hypostatizer, the arriver and the departer, the speaker and the questioner—all are empty. Quiescent nirvana is also completely empty. All regions of space are also empty." (This is the first way.) "In the midst of nothing to seek, I purposely seek this. Where is this true law of the emptiness of emptiness to be sought? It is sought in the six perfections." (This is the second way.)

This is the same as the eighteen emptinesses of the *Great Wisdom Scripture,* no different from the scripture's saying that the city of Kapilavastu is empty, the Buddha is empty, and great nirvana is empty. Applying this knowledge of emptiness to all phenomena, it all becomes seeing.

Transcendent wisdom has four methods, referred to as four entryways into a clear cool pool. The inner truth that is attained is impartial great wisdom. Thus it is universalized by various methods and equal in essence; so it is referred to by the term *universally equal.*

Having one seek the dream kings is an expedient preceding these two contemplations. The place of practice is the sphere of purity. Getting rid of the "chaff" of the five basic afflictions, one reveals the "grain" of reality. This is also "concentration and wisdom used to adorn the spiritual body." The fragrant ointment is unexcelled conduct. The five-colored canopy is analytically seeing the five clusters to avoid bondage and producing great compassion covering the universe. The round altar is the immutable ground of reality. The streamers and pennants are overturning delusions about the realm of reality and producing understanding that stirs one to emancipation. The pennants and the altar are inseparable; that is, stirring to emancipation and not stirring to emancipation are not separate. The incense and lamps are discipline and knowledge. The high seat is the emptiness of all things; all Buddhas abide in this emptiness. The twenty-four images are the conscious knowledge of contemplating the twelve links of conditioning backward and forward. The food offerings are the astringent contemplations of impermanence and suffering, which assist the path. The new clean clothing is tranquil tolerance. The accumulation of the delusion of animosity is called old, overthrowing animosity and producing tolerance is called new. Seven days is the seven branches of enlightenment; one day is the one true reality. Washing three times is seeing one reality, practicing three contemplations, cleaning away three obstacles, and purifying three knowledges. The one teacher is the one true reality. The precepts and meditation on the twelve links of conditioning backward and forward are producing the discipline concomitant with the path. The spells are appropriate transmission.

The *Necklace Scripture* explains that there are ten kinds of twelve links of conditioning. Thus there are one hundred and twenty links; one incantation, one link. In sum, there are only three courses: suffering, action, and affliction. Now, to incant against these causal conditions is to incant against the three courses. In terms of repentance, the phenomenal is repentance of the course of suffering and the course of action, while the noumenal is repentance of the course of affliction. It is written, "If you break the precepts, from those for novices to those for full initiates, it is impossible not to be reborn." This passage relates to repentance of the course of action. "The eyes, ears, and other faculties are purified" is a passage relating to repentance of the course of suffering. "On the seventh day, one sees the Buddhas of the ten directions, hears them teaching, and attains nonregression" is a passage relating to repentance of the course of affliction. When these three obstacles are gone, the tree of the twelve links of conditioning crumbles, and the house of the five clusters is empty. Meditating on reality correctly breaks through these, so it is called the Buddhas' true method of repentance.

As for promotion of practice, the Buddhas all attain enlightenment by this teaching. This is the father and mother of the Buddhas, the supreme treasure of the world. If you can put it into practice, you attain the whole treasure. If you can only recite it, you attain half the treasure. If you make offerings of flowers and incense, you attain a fraction of the treasure. Even Buddha and Manjushri could not fully tell of a fraction of the treasure, much less the half or the whole. If you piled jewels up from the earth to the heavens and offered them to Buddha, that would not match giving a meal to a keeper of the scripture. This is extensively explained in the scriptures.

We also explain the method and promotion of practice according to the *Lotus Scripture*. Method involves what to do and not to do physically, speech and silence, and mental stopping and seeing.

What is to be done involves ten things. First, adorning and purifying the place of practice. Second, purifying the body. Third, offering up the acts of the body, speech, and mind. Fourth, entreating the Buddhas. Fifth, bowing to the Buddhas. Sixth, purifying the six senses. Seventh, circumambulation. Eighth, reciting scripture. Ninth, sitting meditation. Tenth, realization. (There is a separate work called *Dharma Flower Concentration,* written by the teacher of Tian-t'ai. Practitioners base the practice on this. This also includes speech and silence, so these will not be dealt with separately here.)

As for mental stopping and seeing, the *Contemplation of Universal Good* says, "Devoting yourself to recitation of scripture, if you do not enter concentration, then repent of the misdeeds of the six senses six times day and night." The book on peaceful activity in the *Lotus Scripture* says, "Not acting on anything, also not practicing nondiscrimination." The two scriptures are complementary; you should not cling to words and contend. It is simply that because of circumstances they are brought out one after the other; it is not that they are strictly different.

The book on peaceful activity speaks of preserving,

reading and writing, explaining, and earnestly prostrating oneself; are these not phenomena? The scripture on contemplation explains formless repentance: "One's own mind is inherently empty; fault and merit have no owner, the sun of wisdom can melt them away." Is this not noumenon? The teacher of Nanyue spoke of peaceful activity with form and formless peaceful practice; are these not named in terms of phenomena and noumenon?

People who observe this practice cultivate purgation of the six senses by phenomenal practices, to induce entry into realization; therefore it is called formal. If one looks directly into the emptiness of all things as a means, this is called formless. At the time of ineffable realization, both are abandoned. If you get the sense of this, you will have no doubts about the two scriptures.

Now I will go through scriptural passages to cultivate contemplation. When scripture speaks of a six-tusked white elephant, this refers to the uncontaminated six spiritual powers of bodhisattvas. Tusks have the function of sharpness, like the swiftness of the powers. The elephant, with great strength, represents the spiritual body bearing its charge. Noncontamination and nondefilement are symbolized by whiteness. On its head are three people, one holding a diamond mace, one a diamond disk, and one a wish-fulfilling jewel; these represent the three knowledges dwelling in the uncontaminated head. The mace prodding the elephant to walk represents wisdom guiding action. The turning of the disk represents emerging into the conditional. The wish-fulfilling jewel represents the Middle Way.

On the elephant's tusks are ponds, symbolizing the eight liberations, which are the substance of meditation.

The spiritual powers are the function of concentration. The tusks represent both meditation and spiritual powers because substance and function are inseparable. On the tips of the tusks are ponds, in the ponds are lotuses, representing the sublime causes. These causes consist of the use of spiritual powers to purify buddha-lands and benefit sentient beings. The causes come from the powers just as lotuses emerge from ponds. In the blossoms are women, representing compassion. Without objectless compassion, how could it be possible to shrink the body by spiritual powers so that it goes into the world? The powers operate by compassion, just as the blossoms support the women. The women hold musical instruments, representing the four integrative methods. Compassion training the body and speech manifests various forms of cooperation and beneficial action; the two forms of giving, material and spiritual, lead beings in many ways, just as the notes of five hundred musical instruments are infinite. Manifesting pleasing physical form represents the concentration of universal manifestation of the physical body. It appears as is appropriate and appreciated, and not necessarily only as a white jade elephant. The mental command of speech is compassion influencing the speech to explain various doctrines.

All of these are different names for the concentration of the Lotus of Truth. If you get the idea, you can freely construe teachings on the body of the elephant.

As for promoting practice, the *Contemplation of Universal Good* says, "If people have violated precepts and want to eliminate the sins of countless eons of samsara in a trice, if they want to arouse the aspiration for enlightenment and enter nirvana without extinguishing afflictions, if they want to purify the senses without abandoning desire, if they want to see things beyond barriers, if they want to see emanation bodies of Prabhutaratna Buddha and Shakyamuni Buddha, if they want to attain the concentration of the Lotus of Truth and the mental command of all words, if they want to enter the room of Buddha, wear the robe of Buddha, sit on the seat of Buddha, and expound the teachings to all beings, if they want to have the great bodhisattvas like Manjushri and Bhaishajyaguru hover in attendance in the sky holding flowers and incense, then they should practice this *Lotus Scripture,* read and recite the teachings of the Great Vehicle, think about the issue of the Great Vehicle, cause this knowledge of emptiness to unite with the mind, and think of the mother of bodhisattvas. Supreme skill in means is born of pondering the characteristics of reality. Sins are like frost and dew, which the sun of wisdom can melt and evaporate. On accomplishing these things, all will be fulfilled. Those who can hold this scripture can see me, and also see you, and honor Prabhutaratna and the emanation bodies, pleasing the Buddhas." This is expounded at length in the scripture. Who can hear such a teaching and not aspire to enlightenment? Only the unworthy, the foolish, the blind, the ignorant.

The fourth mode is concentration neither walking nor sitting. The preceding modes used only walking and/or sitting; as this one is different from the foregoing, in order to make four terms we have named it neither walking nor sitting, but in reality it includes walking, sitting, and all activities. For this reason, the Teacher of Nanyue called it "according to one's own mentation." When mentation arises, one practices concentration. The *Great Wisdom*

Scripture calls it concentration being aware of mentation, being clearly conscious of all mental processes. Although there are three names, really they are one method.

Now, to interpret the name according to scripture, *awareness* means clear cognition; *mentation* means mental events, states, and processes. Concentration is as explained previously. When mental states arise, the practitioner introspects and does not see movement, root source, final ramifications, where they come from, or where they go. Therefore it is called awareness of mentation. Why do we speak of awareness in reference to mentation? When we search out the source of phenomena, we find all are made by mentation; therefore we begin our discussion with mentation.

Consciousness of objects, which is unlike wood or stone, is called mind. Mental assessment is called mentation. Clearly differentiating cognition is called discriminating consciousness. Such distinctions fall into the delusions of mind, conceptions, and views; how can this be called awareness? What we mean by awareness is clearly knowing it is not that mentation exists in the mind, nor is there no mentation; in the mind there neither is nor is not discriminating consciousness; in mentation there neither is nor is not mind; in mentation there neither is nor is not discriminating consciousness; in discriminating consciousness there neither is nor is not mentation; in discriminating consciousness there neither is nor is not mind. Mind, mentation, and discriminating consciousness are not one, so we set up three terms; yet because they are not three, we speak of one nature. If you know the terms are not terms, then the nature is not nature either.

Not being terms, they are not three; not being nature, they are not one. Not being three, they are not disparate; not being one, they are not merged. Because they do not merge, they are not existent; because they do not disperse, they are not empty. Because they are not existent, they do not perdure; because they are not empty, they do not perish. If you do not see permanence or annihilation, you do not see unity or difference. If you observe mentation, this includes mind and consciousness; everything is like this too. If you break through mentation, ignorance crumbles and the rest of your compulsions all depart. So even though there are many phenomena, we just bring up mentation to explain concentration. By observing we tune and align; therefore it is called concentration aware of mentation. "According to one's own mentation" and "neither walking nor sitting" can be understood along these lines.

Herein there are four types. One is according to scriptures. The second is in reference to virtues. The third is in reference to evils. The fourth is in reference to neutral phenomena.

The scriptural methods of practice that do not belong to the previously explained concentrations belong to concentration according to one's mentation. For the moment I will indicate the forms in terms of entreaty of Avalokiteshvara.

Array a place of practice in a quiet location, with pennants, canopy, incense, and lamps, and enshrine images of Amitabha Buddha and the two bodhisattvas Avalokiteshvara and Mahasthamaprapta in the direction of the west. Provide a toothbrush and clean water. If you go to the toilet, perfume your body. Bathe and put on clean clothing.

Beginning on a day of fasting, face west and prostrate your whole body on the ground, paying obeisance to the Three Treasures, the seven Buddhas, Shakyamuni Buddha and Amitabha Buddha, the three spells, the two bodhisattvas Avalokiteshvara and Mahasthamaprapta, and the host of saints. After prostration, kneel, light incense, and scatter flowers. Meditate most attentively, in the usual manner.

After the offering, sit straight with accurate mindfulness and focus your attention on counting your breaths. Making ten breaths one thought, when you have completed ten thoughts, then rise, light incense, and thrice entreat the supreme Three Treasures for the sake of all beings. After this entreaty, call the names of the Three Treasures three times, and also call the name of Avalokiteshvara. Join your palms and recite the four-stanza verse, and then chant a spell three times, or once, or seven times, depending on how early or late in the day it is.

After the spell chanting, confess and repent, recalling your transgressions. After revealing them and being purged, bow to the objects of the preceding entreaties. Following this, one person gets up on the high seat and either chants or recites relevant scriptural passages, while the rest listen attentively. This is the procedure for the morning and the first part of the night; the rest of the time, the ordinary rites are followed. If it seems insufficient, consult the scriptures for additions to augment it.

Scripture says, "When the eye is involved with forms, how can it be controlled and stabilized? When the mind is involved in clinging to objects, how can it be controlled and stabilized?" The *Great Collection* says, "Mindfulness of thusness is stable." Thusness is emptiness. These scriptures go into reality analytically; this is just a different way of referring to emptiness.

According to scripture, "Earth is not solid." If you say earth exists, existence is substantial, and substantiality means solidity. If you say earth does not exist, or both exists and does not, or neither exists nor does not, these all have the sense of being hard and fast as facts; what is illustrated here is ultimate ungraspability, which undermines the nature of being solid or hard and fast.

When scripture says the nature of water is not stable, it means that if you consider water as existent, existence is stability; and so on. Even if you consider water neither existent nor nonexistent, this is still stability. Now, we do not dwell in the four propositions of existence, nor in the four propositions of nonexistence, nor in inexplicability; that is why scripture says the nature of water is not stable.

Scripture says the nature of wind has no resistance. If you see wind as existent, this is resistance; the same goes for seeing wind as nonexistent, both, and neither. The four propositions of nonexistence do not apply either. Thus it says that the nature of wind has no resistance.

Scripture says the nature of fire is not substantial. Fire does not come from itself, nor from something else, nor from both; nor does it arise without cause. Fundamentally it has no nature of its own; it exists dependent on conditions. Therefore it is called insubstantial.

This is the way it is with contemplation of forms. Sensation, conception, mental patterns, and consciousness each enter reality in the same way. As this is the way the clusters are contemplated, so the twelve links of conditioning are like echoes in a valley, like the pith of a plantain, like dew and lightning, and so on. Exerting these thoughts all at once, causing the contemplation of emptiness to be accomplished, you should exercise diligently and practice it to effect union with it. The basis, contemplative knowledge, is indispensable.

The spell that digests and quells poison can break through the obstacle of retribution. The spell that breaks up evil behavior can break through the obstacle of action. The six-phrase spell can break through the obstacle of afflictions, clear away the roots of the three poisons, and assure attainment of Buddhahood. The six phrases are six Avalokiteshvaras, able to break through the three obstacles of the six states of mundane existence.

The Avalokiteshvara of Great Compassion breaks through the three obstacles of the state of hell. In this state, suffering is grievous, so it is appropriate to use great compassion.

The Avalokiteshvara of Great Benevolence breaks through the three obstacles of the state of hungry ghosts. For the hunger and thirst of this state, it is appropriate to use great benevolence.

The Avalokiteshvara of Lionlike Fearlessness breaks through the three obstacles of the state of animals. The king of beasts being powerful and fierce, it is appropriate to use fearlessness.

The Avalokiteshvara Universally Shining with Great Light breaks through the three obstacles of the state of titans. For the suspicion, envy, jealousy, doubt, and prejudice of this state, it is appropriate to use universal illumination.

Avalokiteshvara the Great Being among Humans and Celestials breaks through the three obstacles of the human state. In the human state are facts and principles:

conquering arrogance and conceit in fact is called celestial or human; seeing the Buddha-nature in principle is called great.

Avalokiteshvara as the Great Brahma, profound and remote, breaks through the three obstacles of the celestial state. Brahma is the chief of celestials, representing the ruler gaining subjects.

Extending the six Avalokiteshvaras, they are twenty-five concentrations. Great compassion is undefiled concentration. Great benevolence is mental pleasure concentration. The lion is nonregressing concentration. The great light is joyful concentration. The great being is four concentrations, such as the phantomlike concentration. The Great Brahma is seventeen concentrations, such as the immovable concentration. If you think on your own, you can see.

This scripture applies to the repentance of people in each of the three vehicles. People who conquer themselves and liberate themselves and destroy their bonds become arhats. If their virtue is greater and their faculties sharp and they contemplate ignorance and the rest of the links of conditioning, they attain the path of awakening to conditioning. If they produce great compassion, their bodies are like crystal, Buddhas visible in their pores, and they attain the heroic progression concentration and abide in nonregression. In the scriptures of the Great Vehicle there are these types. There are also repentances associated with seven Buddhas and eight bodhisattvas, and the repentance of the bodhisattva Space Treasury painting outhouses for eight hundred days. All repentances of this kind are included in concentration according to one's mentation.

Second is contemplation in reference to virtues. This is twofold. First we distinguish four phases, then we go through virtues. First we distinguish the four phases. Consciousness has no form and cannot be seen; we distinguish it in terms of four aspects: before thought, on the verge of thought, in thought, after thought. Before thought refers to when the mind has not yet stirred. The verge of thought refers to when the mind is about to stir. In thought means when focused on an object. After thought means when the focus on an object has passed and is gone. If you can comprehend these four phases, you will enter unity without form.

QUESTION: Both before and after thought there is no mind; therefore they are signless, so how can they be observed?

ANSWER: Before thought, even though the mind has not yet stirred, it is not ultimately nonexistent. It is like when someone has not done something, and then later does something; you cannot say that there is no person before he has acted. If there were no person, who would subsequently act? It is because there is someone who has not yet acted that there can be action. This is the way it is with the mind; because of not yet thinking, there can be the verge of thought. If there were no prethought state, how could there be incipient thought? So even before thought there cannot be ultimately no thought, even though it is not yet existent. After thought, even though it has passed away, it can still be observed. It is like when someone has acted, you cannot say the person does not exist; otherwise, who did the action? The extinction of mind after thought is also like this; it cannot be said to be permanently extinct. If it were permanently extinct, this would be nihilism, with no cause or result. Therefore, even though after thought it is extinct, it still can be observed.

QUESTION: The past is already gone, the future has not yet arrived, and the present does not remain. As there is no mind apart from past, future, and present, what mind does one observe?

ANSWER: Your question is wrong. If the past were eternally extinct, it could not be known at all. If the future, not having yet happened, cannot be known, and the present, not remaining, cannot be known, then how could sages know the mental states of past, present, and future? Even spirits know their own pasts, presents, and futures, as well as those of others; how could practitioners entertain nihilistic views? You should know that even though the mental states of past, present, and future have no fixed reality, they can still be known. Thus a verse says, "What the Buddhas teach is not nihilism, in spite of emptiness; not permanence, in spite of continuity. Sin and virtue do not disappear either. If you are nihilistic, you are like a blind man facing colors; you do not have the eye of right seeing, and you gain nothing."

Once practitioners know the mind has these four aspects, with unattached knowledge they introspectively examine whatever good or bad thoughts the mind produces.

Next is going through virtues. There are many good things, but for the present we will speak in terms of the six perfections. If there are sense objects, we should let go of the six senses. If there are no material things, we should use the six actions. If we discuss both letting go and using, this amounts to twelve things.

First let us speak of the mind in four phases when the eye senses form. There is before seeing, about to see, seeing, and after seeing. These four cannot be seen, yet cannot not be seen. Also look back at the mind aware of form: it does not come from outside, since what comes from outside has nothing to do with oneself; it does not come from within, since what emerges from within does not depend on conditions. Since there is neither inside nor outside, there is no between. It does not perpetually exist of itself, so we must know that what is aware of form is ultimately empty. The form seen is equal to emptiness, and the seer of form is the same as blind. This contemplation applies to the rest of the senses, up to and including the mind focusing on phenomena: the four minds —before focusing, about to focus, focusing, and after focusing—are all ungraspable. Looking back at the mind that is aware of phenomena, you find it does not come from outside or inside. There are no objective phenomena and no objectifier; all are equal to emptiness. This is the contemplation of awareness of the six senses.

The eye faculty, material objects, space and light, each have no perception or discrimination; the combination of these conditions produces the eye consciousness, and the conditional relations of the eye consciousness produce intellectual consciousness. When the intellectual consciousness arises, it can discriminate. Based on the intellectual consciousness, there is visual consciousness, which can see.

Seeing, producing craving, craving coloring objects, then breaking the precepts one has accepted—these are the four phases of hell.

When the mind really is attracted to things but hypocritically denies it, these are the four phases of the state of ghosts.

Becoming attached to things and imagining self and personal possession—these are the four phases of the state of animals.

Thinking in terms of one's own things and others' things, thinking oneself superior to others—these are the four phases of the state of titans.

Giving one's things to others, not taking what is not given, in the material world developing humanity, deference, justice, trustworthiness, intelligence, morality, and virtue—these are the four phases of human and celestial states. Observing the mind in four phases, the arising and vanishing of mental appearances, observing states of mind not remaining, states of mind that are painful, pleasant, or neutral, observing states of mind as having no independence, observing states of mind as being conditioned—these are the four phases of the two vehicles.

Seeing the ills of one's own four phases as such, observing the four phases of others to also be so, one arouses compassion and practices the six perfections. Why? Because the nature and characteristics of the objects of the six senses are like this: for measureless eons we have been stubborn and foolish and have kept clinging to them, unable to relinquish them, or even if we relinquish them, we are unable to forget them. Now, seeing that objects are not objects, there is no reception of objects. Seeing that faculties are not faculties, there is no attachment to self. Seeing that a person cannot be grasped, there is no receiver. The emptiness of these three is called the perfection of giving.

The *Diamond Cutter Scripture* says that if you give while dwelling on form, sound, scent, flavor, texture, or phenomena, then this is called giving dwelling on appearances. This is like entering a dark room and not seeing anything. Giving without dwelling on sound, flavor, and so on, is called formless giving. This is like someone with sight in the daylight clearly seeing all kinds of things.

To speak simply of "not seeing appearances" is elliptic and thus still hard to understand. Not seeing things as having appearances or not having appearances, as both having and not having appearances, leading those attached to appearances here and there out to emancipation and not producing false views, is called formless giving reaching the other shore. All things conduce to giving, making the Great Vehicle. These are the four phases of bodhisattvahood.

Seeing the four phases as equal to space, furthermore, is "eternity." Not feeling the four phases is "bliss." Not producing actions because of the four phases is "self." The inability of the four phases to defile is "purity." These are the four phases of the state of Buddhas.

Thus, although the four phases are empty, within emptiness we see various kinds of four phases. Ultimately seeing innumerable Buddha teachings everywhere, this forms the Great Vehicle. This is the four phases of provisional names.

If they were void, they shouldn't contain the ten universes. The ten universes arise from conditions, and their substance has no existence beyond this. Not being existent, they are empty; not being void, they are existent. Not grasping emptiness or existence, yet simultaneously aware of emptiness and existence, the three truths are evident, and you have the knowledge and vision of Buddha, fully clear in the mind in four phases.

Observing the mind in four phases in the five senses of sound, scent, taste, touch, and phenomena, completely awakening to the three truths, inconceivable, is done in the same way, and since it can be known by following the foregoing methods, I will not record the details here.

Next, reflect on the practice of giving while observing the six actions. Having observed before thinking of acting, on the verge of action, in the process of acting, and in the aftermath of action, you find that the four phases, slow or fast, cannot be grasped; and neither do you see ungraspability. Looking back into the mind that is aware, you find it does not come from outside, does not emerge from inside, is not in between, and does not perpetually exist of itself. There is no action and no actor, so it is ultimately empty and quiescent; yet because of the functioning of the mind, there is coming and going. It may break precepts or fool others or be submissive or be dominant or be just and deferential or be meditative or be tranquil or be loving and compassionate.

Relinquishing the six fields of sense objects yet carrying out the six actions—walking, standing, sitting, reclining, speaking, being silent—expediently coming and going, every step is like an illusion, a phantasm, ethereal, without subject or object. A thousand miles does not seem far, a few steps does not seem near. Whatever you do, the effort is not wasted, and yet you do not hope for reward. Persisting in giving in this way, you accomplish all the innumerable teachings of Buddha, fulfill the Great Vehicle, and reach the Other Shore.

Also contemplate the mind in one phase containing the ten universes. One is not fixed as one, so it can be ten; ten is not fixed as ten, so it can be one. Not one, not ten, yet aware of both one and ten, in a single moment of awareness the three truths are present. Standing, sitting, reclining, speaking, silence, and work are also like this, as can be known along the foregoing lines. Thus the *Lotus of Truth* says, "Also we see bodhisattvas giving away clothing, seeking Buddhahood thereby." This is the same principle.

Hitherto we have discussed giving in terms of twelve things altogether, the six sense fields and the six actions. Now let us discuss the six perfections in reference to each thing.

When practitioners are walking and they observe beings with the eye of great compassion, they do not apprehend the appearance of beings, while beings get freedom from fear from the bodhisattvas; this is giving within walking.

Not harming beings, and not grasping appearances of sin or virtue, is called discipline.

While walking, when thoughts do not arise and there is no movement and no dwelling point, and the clusters, media, and elements are also all unstirring, this is called forbearance.

While walking, not apprehending the movement of the feet, the mind not thinking of what is ahead or conscious of what is past, not aroused, dwelling, or passing away in the midst of all things, is called vigor.

Not apprehending samsara or nirvana in body or mind,

no feelings and thoughts sticking to anything, not savoring, not confused, is called meditation.

While walking, the various parts of the body are like clouds, like reflections, dreams, illusions, echoes, phantasms, without origin or destruction, annihilation or permanence; the clusters, media, and elements are empty and quiescent, with no bondage and no liberation; this is called wisdom.

This is expounded extensively in the *Scripture on Heroic Progress.*

Also, when you are tranquil during walking, which is characteristic of concentration, if you do not see through this you will become addicted to concentration and attached to the taste of meditation. Now observe the concentrated mind; since there isn't even any mind in the mind, where is concentration? You should know this concentration arises from delusion. When you observe in this way and do not see emptiness or nonemptiness, then you break through the characteristics of concentration and do not become attached, and are "born" by skill in expedient means. This is the understanding of bodhisattvas.

Before practitioners are enlightened, they may conceive of themselves as able to observe the mind and, considering this subtle wisdom, become attached to this "wisdom" and become proud. This is called the obstacle of knowledge, which thwarts liberation, just as those on false paths fail to gain liberation. In that case, look back into the observing mind; you do not see any abode, and there is no arising or passing away—ultimately there is no observer or nonobserver. Since there is no observer, then who observes phenomena? Not grasping the observer of mind, you detach from the notion of observing. The

Great Treatise on Wisdom says, "Thoughts, imagination, and contemplation gone, the mind that creates false descriptions vanishes; myriad wrongs removed, the pure mind is always one. Such noble, fine people can thus see transcendent wisdom." This is what the *Great Collection* means by "observe the mind and mentation."

In this way, three concentrations are included in walking. First you see through all kinds of appearances of existence; not seeing inside or outside is empty concentration. The next seeing destroys the appearance of emptiness; this is called signless concentration. The last seeing does not see an agent; this is uncreate concentration. You also break through the threefold delusions of mind, thoughts, and views, as well as the three poisons of greed, hostility, and stupidity, and cross over the realms of desire, form, and formlessness, subdue the four demons, accomplish the perfections, take in the realm of reality, and develop and fulfill all aspects of the Teaching, not just the six perfections and three concentrations. If you fulfill all the teachings in walking, so will it be in the other eleven things.

Next, again going through the six sense fields, striving to be careful and pure, as if carrying a bowl of oil so as not to spill a drop, and in the six actions being dignified and orderly, is just called discipline, the reward of which is elevation and happiness. It is not concentration and is not called perfection. If you attain observant wisdom in respect to the twelve things, discipline will develop of itself. This means observing the mind in four phases: before perceiving, about to perceive, perceiving, after perceiving. Seeing the mind in every way, you do not apprehend the aroused mind, and neither do you apprehend the observing mind. Not inside or outside, it has no going or coming; quiescent, it has no birth or annihilation. (This is first.)

When you are able to see in this way, then body, mouth, and limbs are pure as space. This is keeping the three kinds of precepts regulating behavior, not omitting, not breaking, not transgressing. Breaking through the errant reflections and ruminations of the four phases is keeping the precept of nonadulteration. Not being disturbed by the four phases is keeping the precepts concomitant with concentration. When the four phases do not arise, this is keeping the precepts concomitant with the Path. Discerning the various kinds of four phases without lingering or blockage is keeping the precept of nonattachment. Distinguishing the four phases without error is keeping the precept praised by the wise. Knowing that the four phases include all phenomena is keeping the universalist precept of independence. Knowing the four qualities [eternity, bliss, selfhood, purity] of the four phases is keeping the ultimate precept. (This is second.)

Once the mind is clear and clean, avoiding the two extremes, correctly entering the Middle Way and simultaneously aware of the two truths [of emptiness and conditional existence], the inconceivable realm of Buddhas is fulfilled, without lack. (This is third.)

Consciousness of form, material phenomena, and the perceiver cannot be grasped; when all three are gone, this is giving. The mind being at peace and unperturbed in respect to material form and consciousness of form is called forbearance. Being unstained and unhindered by form and consciousness of form is called vigor. Not being confused by form and consciousness of form is called meditation. Form and consciousness of form are like illusions, like phantasms; this is called wisdom. Form and consciousness of form are like space; this is called empty concentration. Not grasping this emptiness is called signless concentration. Having no subject and no object is called uncreate concentration. Not only the three truths, six perfections, and three emptinesses but all the countless principles and practices of Buddhism can be understood along these lines. Having seen the sense field of material form this way, the same applies to the other five sense fields, and to the six senses and six actions as well. The *Lotus Scripture* says, "We also see bodhisattvas seeking buddhahood by perfection of conduct." This is the same principle.

Next is going through the virtue of forbearance. In terms of both action and sensing, there are unpleasant and pleasant. *Pleasant* means what conforms with one's wishes, *unpleasant* refers to what is counter to one's wishes. As previously explained, here one does not become angry at what is unpleasant or attached to what is pleasant; there is no perception, no perceiver, no action, no agent.

Next is going through the virtue of vigor. Of old it has been said, "Vigor has no particular essence, it is just being diligent in practices," but reasoning in terms of the meaning, it must have a particular essence, just as ignorance permeates all compulsions, and yet there is ignorance itself in addition to the compulsions. For now we will describe vigor in terms of reciting scripture to spur the mind. Not failing to do this day and night, one will attain fluency, but this is not the insight that comes of absorption. Now contemplate the pressures of the breath on points of articulation together producing sound, like echoes, not inside, not outside, no reciter, no recital. Examine it through all the four phases. Not producing a "perceiver" in regard to sense data, not producing an "agency" in regard to objects, afflictions do not intervene in the recitation, and thought after thought flows into the great ocean of nirvana. This is called vigor.

Next is going through the various meditations. The basic meditations, the nine thoughts, the rejections, and so on, are just meditation, not perfection. Observing the four phases in entering concentration, you do not even see mind, so where is concentration? Thus do you arrive at the reality of meditation, and so include all the teachings in meditation. Therefore, in the *Treatise on Wisdom*, after it has explained the eight thoughts, it explains the ten powers, the four fearlessnesses, and all the other qualities of Buddhahood. The professors, not understanding the deep meaning, all say the treatise is mistaken and should not explain these yet. The fact is that the author of the treatise here is explaining the eight thoughts as aspects of the Great Vehicle and therefore extensively explains these qualities.

Next is going through wisdom. The *Treatise on Wisdom* speaks of eight kinds of wisdom. For now speaking in terms of worldly knowledge, using it to observe the six senses and six actions, when we look for worldly knowledge in the four phases, we cannot grasp it. This is all as explained before, and dealing with all other virtues is done in the same way.

QUESTION: If one truth includes all truths, it should be enough to use seeing alone. Why should we use stopping? One perfection would be enough; why use the other five?

ANSWER: The six perfections mutually complete each other. It is like when you enter battle wearing armor, it should all fit together tightly. Seeing is like a lamp, stopping is like a room with no draft. Stopping and seeing are also like washing clothes or cutting hay: in washing clothes, first you use soapy water (stopping), then you use clear water (seeing); in cutting hay, first you hold the hay tightly (stopping), then you cut it (seeing).

Also, wisdom as the reality realm includes everything, and other things are not needed besides; other realities as the reality realm include wisdom, and wisdom is not needed besides.

Also, wisdom is all truths and realities, all truths and realities are wisdom; there is no duality, no distinction.

Third is going through bad things with concentration according to one's mentation. Good and bad have no fixity. For example, the veils are considered bad, while practicing the perfections is considered good; but when the rewards of human and celestial states are exhausted, one falls back into the three mires and again this is bad. Why? As long as the veils and perfections are not transcended, they are all bad. Those in the two vehicles call emancipation from suffering good, but though the two vehicles are good, they can only liberate themselves, and this is not the characteristic of good people. The *Great Treatise* says, "Better to have the heart of a leprous jackal than the mind of the self-liberated." We should know that samsara and nirvana are then both bad; bodhisattvas of the six perfections liberate self and others with benevolence and compassion, and this is then called good. But even though able to liberate self and others, if food is put in a poisoned vessel, the food kills people; then again it is bad, so then cutting off all the three vehicles alike is called good. But then if you fail to see the principle of the separate or special teaching and have not yet ejected ignorance, then again this is bad, and the special teaching is considered good. Yet even though you see the principle of the separate or special teaching, if you still cling to expedients, you cannot harmonize with the noumenon. The major scripture says, "Hitherto we were all called people of erroneous views." Is error not bad? Only the complete teaching is considered good. Good following reality is called the Path; turning away from reality is called not the Path. If you realize the bad is not bad, all is reality; then while traveling on what is not the Path you are in touch with and attain to the Path of Buddhas. If you give rise to attachment on the Path of Buddhas and do not digest the elixir, the Path is no longer the Path.

In discussing good and bad this way, the meaning is common in the sense of applying to all the vehicles; now I will explain good and bad in the context of the special or separate teaching.

Practicing the perfections is good, the veils are bad. Observing virtues has already been explained; now I will explain observation in the midst of evils. When the veils have not ceased even though we have already contemplated good, and afflictions are teeming, always arising, and when we observe others' evils, and they too are infinite, we therefore cultivate the thought of all worlds as unpleasant. Then we do not see good people, and there is no good land. Wrapping themselves up in the evil of the veils, even if they are not totally veiled, people just do what is not good. Some are very stingy and greedy, some very undisciplined or very ill tempered or very lazy, very fond of alcoholic drink. When the disposition is easily taken over, there are sure to be faults. Who has no faults? When mendicants who leave society still have not perfected practice, when lay people feel cravings and do not practice the Path, evil is that portion. Even arhats or saints have remaining habits; how much the more do ordinary people!

If ordinary people give rein to evil veils, when they are defeated and have no hope of ever getting out, they should cultivate observational wisdom in the midst of evil, as in the time of Buddha, when lay people with spouses and children and jobs were all able to attain enlightenment. Angulimalya became more compassionate the more he killed; Jetamali was self-controlled even as he drank alcohol; Vasumitra was chaste even as a courtesan; Devadatta was right even in wrong views. If in the midst of evils there were only evil and no possibility of cultivating the Path, these people would have remained ordinary people forever. Because the Path is there within evils, one can become a sage even though acting out evils.

So we know that evil does not obstruct the Path. And the Path does not prevent evil. A stream enterer had ever mounting lust, Pilingavatsa was still arrogant, Shariputra became angry. What loss or gain was there from the perspective of their noncontamination? Just as light and darkness do not remove each other in space, so is the enlightenment of Buddhas revealed. That is the sense of this.

If people are by nature very greedy and very impure, and even though they try to quell and subdue these characteristics they become more acute, they should just let their inclinations be. Why? If veils do not arise, they cannot practice seeing. It is like when you go fishing with hook and line, if the fish is strong and the line is weak, you cannot fight with the fish to pull it in—you just let it take the bait and let it run with it as far as it will, diving or surfacing. Before long you will be able take it in. The same goes for practicing observation or seeing of the veils. The veils are the bad fish, the observational seeing is the hook and bait. If there is no fish, there is no use for the hook and bait. So long as there are fish, be they many or large, that is fine; just follow them with hook and bait, never giving up, and before long the veils can be overcome.

What is seeing? When desire is about to arise, observe desire carefully. There are four aspects: before desiring, incipient desire, desiring, and after desiring. Is it that incipient desire arises when the state before desire passes away? Is it that incipient desire arises without the state before desire passing away? Is it that incipient desire arises when the state before desire has both passed away and not passed away? Or is it that incipient desire arises when the state before desire has neither passed away nor not passed away?

If the incipient state arises when the prior state has passed away, are that passing away and arising identical or separate? Suppose they are identical—but arising and passing away are mutually opposed. Yet if the arising is separate, that arising has no cause.

If the incipient state arises without the state prior to desire passing away, are they identical or separate? If identical, the arising of the two states happens together, and there would thus be no end. If separate, again the arising has no cause.

If the incipient state arises with the prior state having both passed away and not passed away, if it arises from the passing away, there is no need for the not passing away; if it arises from the not passing away, there is no need for the passing away. How can an indefinite cause produce a definite result? If their actuality is one, yet their natures are mutually contradictory; but if their actualities are different, they do not interrelate.

If incipient desire arises when the state before desire has neither passed away nor not passed away, are the objects of double denial existent or nonexistent? If existent, how can it be called denial? If not, how can nothing produce anything?

Using the four propositions in this way, you do not see incipient desire arising; turning the four propositions around, you do not see the state before desire passing away. The arising of the incipient state, the nonarising, both arising and not arising, neither arising nor not arising, are also as explained above.

Seeing the veil of desire as ultimately empty, while simultaneously being aware of both its emptiness and conditional existence, is as explained above. This is called the hook and bait. As long as veils continue to arise, the seeing continues to illuminate; you neither see arising nor see illumination, yet seeing illumines whenever there is arising. (This is the first procedure.)

Also see into what sense field this veil arises from. Is it

from form, or from other sense fields? From what action does it arise? Is it from walking or from other actions?

If it is based on form, is it before seeing, about to see, seeing, or after seeing? If it is based on walking, is it before doing it, about to do it, doing it, or after doing it? For what does it arise? For breaking precepts? For gaining followers? For deception? For jealousy? For humaneness and deference? For good meditation? For nirvana? For the four qualities of the spiritual body? For the six perfections? For the three concentrations? For the innumerable aspects of Buddhahood? (This is the second procedure.)

When you see in this way, there is no receiver of data and no objectifier, yet the reception of sense data and the focusing of sense faculties on objects are both illumined clearly. Phantasms, emptiness, and the nature of reality do not obstruct each other. Why? If the veils obstructed the nature of reality, the nature of reality would break down; if the nature of reality obstructed veils, the veils would not arise. So we know that the veils are none other than the nature of reality; when the veils arise, the nature of reality arises, and when the veils cease, the nature of reality ceases. The *Scripture on Absence of Conformations* says, "Desire is the Path, and so are anger and folly. All Buddhist teachings are in these three things. If people seek enlightenment apart from desire, they are as far from it as the sky is from the earth. Desire is none other than enlightenment."

The *Pure Name Scripture* says, "While traveling on false paths one realizes the Path of Buddhas. All beings are the appearance of enlightenment, and it cannot be further attained; all beings are the appearance of nirvana, and it cannot be further extinguished." For the conceited, detachment from lust, anger, and folly is called liberation; for those without conceit, it is said that the essence of lust, anger, and folly is itself liberation. All passions are seeds of enlightenment; the mountains and seas, form and flavor, are nothing else. This is the inconceivable principle of observing evils. (This is the third procedure.)

Constantly cultivating observational wisdom, uniting with the noumenon of the veils, like form and shadow, is called the stage of contemplative practice. Being able to avoid deviating from true contemplation in the midst of all bad things and worldly occupations is the stage of conformity. Advancing into the rank of the bronze wheel, breaking the root of the veils—the root is ignorance, and when the root is broken down the branches snap—and revealing the Buddha-nature is the stage of partial realization of reality. Finally, when Buddhas exhaust the source of the veils, that is called the ultimate stage. Within the veil of desire are vertically contained the six identities and horizontally contained the six perfections. All things follow this pattern.

Next observe the veil of anger. If people have a lot of anger, depression and excitement successively arise all the time. When they try to stop it, they cannot stop it; when they try to suppress it, they cannot suppress it. They should let it arise as it will and view it by stopping and seeing. Observe the four aspects: where does anger come from? If you cannot grasp its origin, you cannot grasp its passing away either. Who is angry? Who is the object of anger? When you see in this way, you cannot grasp anger; the traces of its coming and going, and its appearances, are empty and quiescent. Seeing the ten states of existence in anger and seeing the four qualities in anger are done as explained above. This is realizing the Path of Buddhas while on the wrong path of anger. Seeing the veils of misconduct, laziness, distraction, error, and folly, as well as all other bad things, is done in the same way.

The fourth procedure is seeing that which is neither good nor bad. These are neutral, undefined things. The reason they should be observed is that some people by nature do not do good or bad, and thus otherwise would have no way to practice meditation according to mentation and would have no means of emancipation from the world. The *Great Treatise* says, "In the neutral there is the perfection of wisdom," so you can cultivate seeing.

Reflect whether the neutral is different from good and bad, or is the same. If the same, it is not neutral. If different, is it that the neutral arises when the nonneutral passes away, or does the neutral arise without the nonneutral passing away, or does the neutral arise while the nonneutral both passes away and does not pass away, or does the neutral arise while the nonneutral neither passes away nor does not pass away? Looking for the nonneutral, you cannot grasp it; so how could you grasp the neutral? Is it the same as the nonneutral, or different? Because it is not the same, they do not combine; because it is not different, they do not separate. Because of noncombination, it does not become; because of nonseparation, it does not pass away.

Also go through the twelve things. Where does the neutral arise? For whom does the neutral arise? Who considers it neutral? When you see it in this way, it is like space.

Also, one neutral thing produces the ten states of being and all phenomena. The neutral is also identical to the nature of reality. The eternal quiescence of the nature of reality is the meaning of stopping. Perpetual illumination while quiescent is the meaning of seeing. You realize the path of Buddhas while on a neutral wrong path; the neutral is the realm of reality, horizontally taking in all things, vertically taking in the six stages, complete in loftiness and breadth. This follows the pattern explained above.

Also, to just explain concentration according to mentation in terms of the final good is the gradual meaning; to explain concentration according to mentation in terms of both good and bad is the sudden meaning; to explain concentration according to mentation in terms of multiple levels of good is the unfixed meaning.

To proceed: the methods of the four kinds of concentration are different, but the insight into noumenon is the same. It is just that the first three methods produce many aids to the Path and also dislodge obstacles to the Path, while concentration according to mentation, having few techniques, produces few of these things. If you just understand the aids to the Path produced by the methods, the formal aspects cannot be comprehensive, but if you understand noumenal seeing, all phenomena are comprehended. Furthermore, if you do not get the sense of noumenal seeing, the formal aids to the Path do not develop either; but if you get the sense of noumenal seeing, concentration in its formal aspects will spontaneously develop. If you practice the Path formally, you can do the mental exercises in a special place, but not outside; meditation according to individual mentation, on the other hand, has no such barriers. Formal methods are limited to the first three, but noumenal insight is common to all four.

QUESTION: There was promotion of practice of the first three concentrations; why is there none for this last one alone?

ANSWER: The wrong paths of the six veils are identical to the Path of liberation. Those of dull faculties, whose obstacles are heavy, sink when they have heard this; if we go on to exhort them to practice, they will lose the meaning even more. North of the Huai River there are people who practice the emptiness of the Great Vehicle and have no qualms about grabbing the snake of passion.

Now I will tell you about them to illustrate this point. Their past teachers had practiced contemplation in respect to virtues for a long time without success, so they let their minds go and practiced contemplation in bad things. They then achieved a little bit of concentration and developed a slight understanding of emptiness. Not discerning people's faculties and conditions, not arriving at the Buddha's meaning, they simply taught others this method alone. After teaching others for a long time, they found one or two people who got some benefit—just as insects chewing wood may happen to form the pattern of a letter—and considered this proof that this alone is true and everything else is false. They laughed at those who kept the precepts and cultivated good, saying that this is not the Path; they simply taught people to do bad things. The blind did not distinguish right and wrong; their spiritual faculties blunt, their afflictions heavy, when they heard this teaching they followed their passions. Believing in and following this, they abandoned the precepts and did anything they wanted to do. Their evils piled up, until the common people, as a result, became contemptuous of them, and the government therefore stamped out Buddhism. This poison has gone deep and to this day has not yet been corrected.

Historical documents say that in the decline of the Chou dynasty there were people with disheveled hair and bare shoulders who did not act according to the rites and manners; eventually foreigners invaded the country again and again, and the dynasty gradually came to an end. Juan Chi, a distinguished intellectual, also went about disheveled, and the scions of aristocrats later imitated him; those who engaged in mutual degradation were considered to have become natural, while those who struggled to regulate themselves were called bumpkins. This was a sign of the end of the leading Ssu-ma clan. The destruction of Buddhist establishments by Yu Wen was also due to the devilish work of Yuan Sung, who urged Yu Wen to believe in omens; Yuan Sung was an evil influence in the destruction of Buddhism and an evil influence in the age.

This has nothing to do with meditation according to individual mentation. Why? Ignorant people like this, with no intelligence or understanding, believe their teachers and look up to their predecessors, thinking this must be the Path. They find it easy, furthermore, to go along with feelings; indulging their minds and grasping comfort, they do not change their delusion. This is like the ancient story of a beautiful woman who had an affliction of the heart and used to frown and groan a lot, paradoxically making her charms all the more beautiful. The woman next door, who was homely to begin with, used to imitate this frowning and groaning, but the only effect was to make her uglier.

The poor travel afar, the rich stay at home; those who rest hide deep, those who fly soar high. The people who indulge in what is bad are like those examples from history; crazy dogs chasing thunder, they create hellish karma. How pitiful! Indulging their desires, unable to stop themselves, they are like flies stuck in spittle.

The faults of these vagabonds are, in brief, like that; the faults of their teachers is in not discerning people's faculties and natures and not understanding the intention of Buddha. The reason Buddha said desire is itself the path is that the Buddha saw the requirements of the situation and knew there was a kind of people who were base and lacking in character and would certainly not be able to practice the Path in good states and actions, and if left to their evildoings would go on compulsively without end; so he had them cultivate stopping and seeing in the midst of desire. He used this teaching as an unavoidable last resort.

It is like when parents see their child afflicted with an illness that is not amenable to any other remedy, and have to knock out the child's teeth to pour a powerful medicine down the child's throat. Once the medicine is ingested, the sickness abates. In the same way, Buddha taught according to potentiality; if it is a good horse, it takes to the right road on merely seeing the shadow of the whip. Such was the Buddha's intention in saying that desire itself is the Path. If there are people for whom it is not suitable to cultivate stopping and seeing in the midst of evils, the Buddha says that virtues are the Path.

The Buddha has both teachings, so why do you repudiate the good and take to the bad? If you are right, you are better than Buddha. You publicly stand before the

Buddha and clearly oppose him. Furthermore, when oppression arises because of the times and, constrained by political affairs, it is not possible to do good works, then we are taught to cultivate stopping and seeing in the midst of evil. Now you are not oppressed or constrained; why do you only use a medicament that poisons others' spiritual life?

Thus in the Agama scriptures it says that a herdsman knows the good fording place and so enables the cattle to cross the river in safety. If something happens to the good place, in an emergency he has to go by a bad ford. Because there are many dangers in the bad ford, hardly any cattle cross over safely. Now you have safely arrived at a good ford, driving your cattle over a good road; why sink yourself and others by taking the bad way? Destroying Buddhism, damaging its prestige, the error affects other people. Such is the fault of bad teachers who do not realize the Buddha's meaning.

It is possible, moreover, to pass both safe and dangerous roads; it is when there is a problem with the safe one that we go by the dangerous one. Good and bad both have a way through; it is after careful consideration of potential that one enters the veils. You who abandon good and are devoted to what is bad—if you can pass through wrong paths, why not walk on water and fire, or go through mountains and walls? You cannot even get through dangerous roads in the world, much less understand the right path while doing what is bad.

Also, you are unable to recognize the conditions of people's faculties. Even one person's inclinations are not fixed, sometimes liking the good, sometimes liking the bad; how much more diverse and varied are the faculties of innumerable people. And yet you simply teach them in terms of desire.

Vimalakirti said, "I think Buddhist disciples who do not observe people's faculties should not teach." Even those of the two vehicles, unobservant, still make mistakes about potentiality; how much the more so you who are blind and follow your own mentalities. This is deviating from scripture, not dealing appropriately with the reality of potentialities. How have stupidity and delusion come to this? If one sees people who teach this without knowing what is appropriate for specific potentials, these are corpses in the ocean of self-discipline and should be ejected, according to the rules. Do not let poison trees grow on a plantation.

Furthermore, when we examine the bad actions of such people, we find bias therein. They say desire is the Path, and demean all women, yet they cannot kill all men on the grounds that anger is the Path. They only like the feeling of smoothness as the Path, but fear the feeling of beating and abrasion, as though there were no Path there. One they practice, one they do not; in one there is the Path, in one there is not. Ignorant and blind, they only practice what causes defilement and harm; they are like corpses littering a flower garden.

The foregoing illustrates the manner in which I criticize people's one-sided practice. If they are confronted with water, fire, swords, or cudgels, they are silent, or they may answer, "You don't see—I am always able to enter," shameless words that contradict their state of mind. They do not get the meaning of the six identities either.

The reason it is necessary to explain this is that it is difficult to strive at the first three methods of practice, so encouragement is needed. Meditation according to individual mentation, adaptively entering evil, seems easy at first, so caution is necessary. It is like when you take a powerful serum, you must have antiserum ready to mitigate it.

QUESTION: In the correct contemplation of the Middle Way, it is enough to practice by unifying the mind; why go to all the fuss and bother of four kinds of concentration going through virtues and evils, appying meditation to twelve things? When the water is muddy, the jewel is obscured; when there is much wind, the waves lap. What benefit is this for clarity and tranquillity?

ANSWER: This is like when a pauper gets a little, he considers it enough and does not wish for anything better. If you contemplate the mind in only one way, what can you do about variation in the mind? This is a failing in your own practice, and if you use it to teach others, well, the faculties and natures of others are different; since even one person's afflictions are countless, needless to say those of many people are innumerable. It is like a physician gathering all kinds of medicine to apply to all kinds of diseases. One kind of patient needs one kind of medicine to cure one kind of disease, but would you think it strange that the physician has many medicines? Your question is like this. The mental diseases of afflictions are countless and boundless. As for one person, so for many.

How is it for one person? If someone wants to hear about the four kinds of concentration and is glad to hear about them, you should explain them all; this is the aim of the world. If from hearing about them a person is able to develop good qualities through gradual practice, then explain all four; this is the aim of individually helping a person. If a person needs constant sitting to cure ills, or constant walking, or half sitting and half walking, or needs concentration according to mentation to cure ills, this is called the aim of specific cure. If a person requires all four methods and attains enlightenment, this is the aim of the ultimate truth. If it is necessary to explain all four even for one person, how could we not use them?

Suppose it is for many people; one person may like constant sitting and not want to do the other three modes, while another may want to do constant walking and not like the other three modes. Adjusting to everyone's inclinations is the aim of the world. The other three aims are also like this.

Each kind of concentration also includes the sense of the four aims. If you enjoy walking, then walk; if you enjoy sitting, then sit. If good qualities develop when walking and you penetrate the teachings, then you should walk. If your mind is clear and cool, joyful and comfortable when sitting, then you should sit. If you are torpid when sitting, you should walk to arouse yourself; if you are distracted and tired when walking, then you should sit. If you are light, empty, and tranquil when walking, then you should walk; if you are peaceful, clear, and sharp when sitting, then you should sit. The other three follow this pattern.

QUESTION: Goodness complements principle and is suitable for cultivating stopping and seeing. Since evil is contrary to principle, how can you cultivate stopping and seeing in its midst?

ANSWER: The *Great Treatise* explains that there are four grades of faculties and obstructions. First is keen faculties without obstruction. Second is sharp faculties with obstruction. Third is dull faculties without obstruction. Fourth is dull faculties with obstruction.

The first kind is superior. People like Shariputra in the time of Buddha were like this. When practitioners practice stopping and seeing in the midst of virtues, because they strive to cultivate virtues they will have no obstructions in the future, while constantly practicing stopping and seeing makes their faculties keen. If one has fulfilled these both in the past, then in the present life one will attain realization with little practice, and progress from the stage of contemplation practice into conformative and true realization. Those who do not enter in this life have not fulfilled the requirements in the past. Cultivation based on good in the present will cause speedy entry in the future.

The next kind are those whose faculties for enlightenment are keen but who are heavily obstructed by accumulated wrongdoing. Such people are represented by King Ajatashatru and Angulimalya of the Buddha's time. Heavily obstructed by their crimes, they should have entered hell, but because they saw the Buddha and heard the Teaching, they woke up and became sages. Because their faculties were keen, their obstructions could not impede them. This is the meaning of people in the present practicing stopping and seeing in the midst of bad conditions; because of creating evil, they will have obstructions in the future, but because of practicing stopping and seeing, their faculties will be sharp. If they meet knowing teachers, they will be prodded into the right path; so how can you say that evil goes against principle and does not permit the practice of stopping and seeing?

Next, those of dull faculties without obstruction are exemplified by Chudapanthaka of the Buddha's time. Although he was without fault in thought, word, and deed, he was by nature extremely dull witted. He repeated a children's verse for ninety days, and this is how he attained sainthood. If intelligent people do not do any evil in thought, word, or deed, if they always keep presence of mind and are not attached to desires and do not undertake useless worldly mortification practices, though they keep the precepts and practice virtue in the present, if they do not practice stopping and seeing, in the future it will be very hard for them to become enlightened even though they will have no obstructions.

The last description is of all evildoers who also do not practice stopping and seeing. Because they do not practice stopping and seeing, they do not attain enlightenment; their faculties are so dull that they do not understand something even when it is explained a thousand times, and they are obstructed in myriad ways because they do much evil. They are like lepers whose bodies have become numb and do not feel a needle even when stuck all the way in to the bone. They just wrap themselves up in evils.

So in these terms, although virtue assists principle, the Path comes from stopping and seeing. Although evil goes against principle, if the faculties are sharp it is possible to break through obstruction. The Path alone is of greatest importance; how could it be proper to give up stopping and seeing because of evil? The major scripture says, "Those lax in discipline are not called lax; it is those lax in the vehicle of enlightenment who are called lax." To thoroughly clarify the four permutations of laxness and diligence, align them with the foregoing explanation of faculties and obstruction. This is also what the scripture means when it says, "It is better to be a Devadatta than an Udraka-Ramaputra." You should diligently listen, reflect, and practice, without letting up, being like the drunken Brahman who shaved his head, the harlot who put on religious garb.

Explaining This Stopping and Seeing to Clarify the Pure Great Rewards of Bodhisattvas

If practice deviates from the Middle Way, it will result in either extreme as a consequence. If practice accords with the Middle Way, there will be superior rewards. Even if you do not yet get out of individual birth and death, the glorious reward is still different from the seven expedient stages; how much the more superior is the true reward. This is represented by a city of fragrance with seven bridges. This will be explained extensively later.

QUESTION: In the teaching of the process of meditation, cultivation and realization are explained; how is this the same as, or different from, this reward?

ANSWER: Cultivation means practice, realization means attainment. Also, cultivation means practicing the cause, realization means learning the effect. These can be attained in the present life. The reward I am talking about now is in the future life. This is the difference. The two lesser vehicles only have the results of practice, they do not have the reward; the Great Vehicle has both.

Explaining This Stopping and Seeing to Connect with the Scriptures and Treatises Rending the Great Net of Delusion

If people skillfully use stopping and seeing to observe the mind, then their insight will be clear and they will comprehend the sudden and gradual teachings, like breaking open an atom and producing a scripture as extensive as the universe; the myriad teachings of Buddha will be clear within one mind. If one wishes to go out and help people, setting up teachings according to potentials, teaching adaptively according to people's capacities, eventually to attain Buddhahood and transform people, one may expound the sudden and gradual teachings as a spiritual sovereign or as a bodhisattva or as a *shravaka*, celestial being, demon, ghost, or in any of the forms of the ten states of being, responsively preaching and inspiring. Or one may extensively explain the sudden and gradual in reply to a questioning by a Buddha, or one may take an opportunity to question a Buddha and elicit the sudden and gradual teachings in response. This will be more fully explained later on.

Explaining This Stopping and Seeing to Return to the Great Abode, the Ultimate Emptiness of All Things

Sticky hands easily get stuck; sleepers and dreamers are hard to awaken. People cling to writings that please them and think they are right; competitively holding on to shards and pebbles, they think these are crystal jewels. They do not even understand obvious sayings about things near at hand; how could they not be confused by esoteric teachings of remote principles? For this reason, we need to discuss the intended goal.

As for the meaning of "intended goal," the "intention" of a writing is what it is getting at, just as rivers flow toward the ocean and flames rise toward the sky. Those who know the secrets and comprehend the profundities without lingering in thought, like a wise minister understanding the inner intention of the king's words, comprehending whatever is expounded and reaching the stage of all knowledge, are those who understand the intended goal. The intention is to go to the three attributes oneself; the goal is to lead others into the three attributes too; therefore it is called the intended goal. Entering into the three attributes oneself is also called the goal, while introducing others into the three attributes is called the intention; thus it is called the intended goal.

Now, to further clarify the intended goal in general and in particular, the Buddhas appear in the world for one great cause, manifest various forms, and let all sentient beings see the body of reality. After beings have seen the body of reality, Buddhas and sentient beings both return to the body of reality. Buddhas also expound various doctrines to enable sentient beings to consummate the omni-science of the enlightened. Once they are endowed with omni-science, Buddhas and sentient beings both return to wisdom. Buddhas also manifest various expedient spiritual powers and miraculous displays to untie all bonds, not letting one person attain extinction alone, extinguishing all with the extinction of those who realize thusness. After extinction, Buddhas and sentient beings both return to liberation. The major scripture says, "Placing you all in the secret treasury, I too before long will dwell there myself." This is called the intended goal in its general aspect.

As for the particularized aspect, there are three kinds of body: the material body, the body of teachings, and the body of truth. If we speak of the end in terms of the cessation of teaching activity, the material body returns to liberation, the body of teachings returns to wisdom, and the body of truth returns to the reality body. There are three kinds of explanation of wisdom: one is explanation of the knowledge of the modes of the Path, the second is explanation of universal knowledge, and the third is explanation of omni-science, knowledge of all particulars. If we speak of the end in terms of the cessation of teaching activity, knowledge of the modes of the Path returns to liberation, universal knowledge returns to wisdom, and knowledge of all particulars returns to the reality body. There are three kinds of liberation: one is untying the bond of nescience, the second is untying the bond of grasping and clinging to appearances, the third is untying the bond of ignorance. When the teaching activity ceases and returns to reality, untying the bond of nescience returns to liberation, untying the bond of grasping appearances returns to wisdom, and untying the bond of ignorance returns to the body of reality. In this sense, the intended goal in its particularized aspect also ends up back in the secret treasury of the three attributes of liberation, wisdom, and reality.

The three attributes, furthermore, are neither three nor one; they are inconceivable. Why? If you say the reality body is just the reality body, that is not the reality body; you should realize the reality body is both a body and not a body, neither a body nor not a body. Abiding in the heroic progression concentration, it variously manifests myriad physical forms, so it is called a body; when its tasks are done, it returns to wisdom. Knowledge is aware that material forms are immaterial, so it is referred to as not a body; when its tasks are done, it returns to wisdom. The body of truth is not the body of material form nor the body of teachings; therefore it is neither a body nor not a body; when its tasks are done, it returns to the reality body. Realizing these bodies are neither the same nor different is called the goal; explaining that these three bodies are neither the same nor different is called the intent. Both enter the secret treasury, hence the name intended goal.

If you say wisdom is just wisdom, that is not wisdom. You should know that wisdom is both knowledge and not knowledge, and it is neither knowledge nor not knowledge. The wisdom of the knowledge of modes of the path knows conventional reality, so it is called knowledge; when its tasks are done, it returns to liberation. The wisdom of universal knowledge knows ultimate truth, so it is called not knowledge; when its tasks are done, it returns to wisdom. The wisdom of knowledge of all particulars knows the mean, so it is called neither knowledge nor not knowledge; when its tasks are done, it returns to the reality body. Realizing that the three wisdoms are neither the same nor different is called the goal; explaining how the three wisdoms are neither the same nor different is called the intent. Both enter the secret treasury, hence the name intended goal.

If you say liberation is just liberation, that is not liberation. You should know liberation is both liberation and not liberation, and it is neither liberation nor not liberation. The liberation of expedient purification trains sentient beings not to be defiled; therefore it is called liberation. When the task is done, it returns to liberation. In the liberation of complete purification, one does not see any sign of sentient beings, or of liberation; therefore it is called not liberation. When the task is done, it returns to wisdom. The liberation of inherent purity is neither liberation nor not liberation; when the task is done, it returns to the body of reality. In terms of realization or explanation, these three liberations are neither the same nor different; all enter the secret treasury, hence the name intended goal.

Furthermore, the three attributes are neither new nor old, yet they are both new and old. Why? Three obstacles screen the three attributes: ignorance screens the body of reality, grasping appearances screens wisdom, and nescience screens liberation. The preexistence of these three obstacles is called old. When the three attributes break through the three obstacles, they are called new because they are now manifest for the first time. The three obstacles are the three attributes, the three attributes are the three obstacles: as the three obstacles are the three attributes, the three obstacles are not old; as the three attributes are the three obstacles, the three attributes are not new. Not new yet new, there are therefore the three attributes as attained by inspiration for enlightenment, up to the three attributes as attained by ultimate realization. Not old yet old, there are therefore the three obstacles overcome by inspiration for enlightenment, up to the three obstacles overcome by ultimate realization. New is not new, old is not old; therefore there are the three attributes of inner essence. If you realize overall that the three attributes are not new, not old, yet new and old, and are not the same or different, and also explain it thus to others, this is the intended goal, in the secret treasury.

Also, in respect to explanation, ignorance already there is called old, the body of reality as illumination breaking through ignorance is called new. Ignorance is illumination, illumination is ignorance: ignorance being illumination, ignorance is not old; illumination being ignorance, illumination is not new. Grasping appearances already there is called old, signlessness breaking through appearances is called new. Appearances are signless, signlessness none other than appearances; what is new, what is old? Nescience already there is called old, knowledge breaking through nescience is called new. Nescience being knowledge, knowledge being nescience, what is new, what is old? If you realize, in general and particular, how new and old are neither the same nor different, and explain it to others this way, this is called the intended goal, entering the secret treasury.

Vertical and horizontal, analysis and synthesis, beginning and end, all follow this pattern.

The intended goal, furthermore, is also like this: that is, the intention is not the intention, yet not not the intention; the goal is not the goal, yet not not the goal. Each must enter the secret treasury; this can be understood on the foregoing model. Because the intention is one's own practice, it is not the intention; because it is teaching others, it is neither the intention nor not the intention, since there is no self and other.

The quiescence of the three attributes of the intended goal being thus, what terms can be used to explain? We don't know what to name it, so we impose such terms as the Middle Way, truth, the body of reality, and neither cessation nor contemplation; we also impose such names as the knowledge of all particulars, impartial great wisdom, and seeing by perfect wisdom; we also impose such names as the heroic progress concentration, great ultimate nirvana, and stopping by inconceivable liberation. You should know the various characteristics, various explanations, and various spiritual powers each enters into the secret treasury. What is the intended goal? Where is the intended goal? Who is the intended goal? The path of speech ends, the course of mind dies out; eternally quiescent as space, this is the intended goal.

Analyzing the Name of Stopping and Seeing

The general outline of the great road is as explained above; what then is the significance of establishing the names of stopping and seeing? Overall, there are four meanings: relative, absolute, uniting differences, and comprehending the three attributes.

First, in the relative sense, stopping and seeing each have three meanings. Stopping has the meanings of cessation, stationing, and stopping in contrast to not stopping. Cessation means that wrong attention and consideration, errant thoughts, and conceptual thinking quietly cease. The *Pure Name Scripture* says, "What is clinging to objects? It means clinging to the triple world. What is ceasing clinging to objects? It means the mind does not grasp anything." This name is applied in reference to what is broken through; this is the meaning of stopping as cessation.

As for the meaning of stationing, this is focusing the mind on true principles, keeping presence of mind stationary, not moving. The *Benevolent King Scripture* says, "Wisdom penetrating noumenon is called stabilization." The *Great Wisdom Scripture* says, "By nondwelling, one dwells in the perfection of wisdom." This name is applied in reference to the stopper; this is the meaning of stopping as stationing.

As for explaining stopping in contrast to not stopping, although the word is the same as above, the meaning is eternally different. Why? In the foregoing two definitions of stopping, we speak of cessational stopping in reference to nirvana, in opposition to the flow of samsara; when the mind courses outside of truth, we speak of stationing stopping in reference to wisdom. Those two generally refer to relation in terms of knowledge and annihilation; this last one particularly refers to relation in terms of truth. Ignorance is the nature of reality, the nature of reality is ignorance; ignorance is not stopping, and it is also not nonstopping, yet we call ignorance not stopping. The nature of reality is also not stopping or nonstopping, yet we call the nature of reality stopping. This is calling the nature of reality stopping in opposition to the nonstopping of ignorance.

Seeing also has three meanings: the meaning of piercing, the meaning of perceptive realization, and the meaning of seeing in contrast to nonseeing. The meaning of piercing is that the sharp function of knowledge pierces and obliterates afflictions. The major scripture says, "The sharp hoe cuts through earth, rocks, and stones, right down to adamant." The *Lotus Scripture* says, "Drilling on the high plateau, you still see dry earth; if you keep on working, eventually you will gradually reach mud." This name is applied in reference to what is broken through, defining seeing as piercing.

The meaning of perceptive realization is that the realization of perceptual knowledge meets with true thusness. The *Auspicious Response Scripture* says, "One is called a contemplative because of stopping the mind and realizing the source." The *Great Wisdom* treatise says, "When the pure mind is always unified, one can perceive wisdom." This name is applied in reference to the seer, thus defining seeing as perceptive realization.

As for seeing in contrast to not seeing, although the word is the same as above, the meaning is different. In the above two aspects of seeing, in general we speak of piercing as opposed to the impenetrability of samsara, and speak of perceptive realization as opposed to the blindness of delusion. Those two generally explain seeing relatively, in terms of knowledge and annihilation; this last one does so particularly, in terms of truth. Ignorance is the nature of reality, the nature of reality is ignorance: ignorance is neither seeing nor not seeing, but we call ignorance not seeing; the nature of reality too is neither seeing nor not seeing, but we call the nature of reality seeing. As scripture says, "The nature of reality is neither light nor darkness, but we call the nature of reality light; emptiness of ultimate reality is neither wisdom nor folly, yet we call ultimate emptiness wisdom." This is explaining seeing in contrast to not seeing.

Thus stopping and seeing both get their names from three meanings.

Second, to explain stopping and seeing absolutely breaks through the preceding three aspects of relative stopping and seeing. First we will break through horizontally, then vertically.

If cessational stopping gets its name from what is broken through, as illumining the object is the main point and removing confusion is auxiliary, since it gets its name from what it detaches from, the name is established from the auxiliary, and so falls into otherness.

If stationing stopping gets its name from the stopper, as illumining the object is the main point and removing confusion is auxiliary, since we speak of the illuminator, the name arises from knowledge and thus falls into selfhood.

If it is not stopping due to cessation of erroneous thought and not stopping due to dwelling on truth, but stopping caused by knowledge and annihilation, the name comes from a combination, and thus falls into collectivity.

If we speak of stopping not in terms of what is broken through or of what breaks through, this falls into causelessness.

Therefore Nagarjuna said, "Phenomena are not born of themselves, nor are they born of another, nor collectively, nor without cause. Therefore they are said to be unborn." How could birthless stopping and seeing be named from any of the four propositions?

What is named based on the four propositions is based on relation, and can be conceived and explained. This birth of bondage and delusion can be broken through and destroyed; how can originating and perishing birth in flux be called stationary stopping? How can the birth of delusion and error be called perceptive realization?

Also, to break through vertically: that which is born from the four propositions is the birth of birth; it is not stopping and seeing. If you can stop views and thoughts and dwell on ultimate truth, this is just talking about the stopping and seeing of birth being unborn in contrast to the birth of birth. If you enter into the conditional with empty mind, stop the delusions as numerous as dust motes and sand grains, and dwell on the worldly truth, this is just talking about the stopping and seeing of unborn birth in contrast to the nonbirth of birth. If you stop ignorance and station the mind on the Middle Way, this is just talking about stopping and seeing in opposition to the nonstopping of the two extremes of samsara and nirvana.

All of these are relative and conceivable. Giving birth to bondage and delusion can be broken through and destroyed, yet this still is not stopping, much less not stopping; it still is not seeing, much less not seeing. Why?

Because clinging has not been done away with entirely, because the path of verbalization is not yet ended, because the results of action are not ended.

Now when we speak of absolute stopping and seeing, we mean obliterating all relativity, horizontal and vertical, obliterating all conceptualizations, obliterating all afflictions, obliterating all actions and all results, obliterating all doctrines, contemplations, experiences, and so on. As all are unborn, it is called stopping, and stopping cannot be grasped. Seeing merges with the object; since the object is quiescent and pure, there is not even any purity, so how could there be seeing? Since there is not even any stopping and seeing, how could we speak of stopping and seeing in contrast to not stopping and seeing, or speak of not stopping and seeing in contrast to stopping and seeing, or speak of neither stopping nor not stopping in contrast to stopping and not stopping? Thus we know stopping and not stopping are both ungraspable; neither stopping nor not stopping is also ungraspable. Since oppositions are eliminated, it is not created. It cannot be thought of in terms of the four propositions, therefore it is not in the province of verbalization, not in the realm of intellectual knowledge. Since there is no name or form, bondage and delusion do not arise; thus there is no samsara, so it cannot be destroyed. Annihilating extinction, extinguishing annihilation, it is therefore called absolute stopping; because erroneous ideas end, it is called absolute seeing.

This is also stopping and seeing entirely without artifice, stopping and seeing without birth and death. Absolute stopping and seeing thus cannot be explained, but if there exist the conditions for the four aims, it can therefore be explained. If there are conditions for the aim of the world, then one explains by uniting differences. If there are conditions for the aim of helping people, then one explains in connection with the three attributes. If there are conditions for the aim of specific cure, then one explains relatively. If there are conditions for the aim of ultimate truth, then one explains absolutely.

While we explain it as stopping and seeing, this name is not inside, outside, or in between, and it also does not always exist of itself. This name does not abide, yet it does not not abide. This name is not in the four propositions in time, or the four propositions in space, therefore we say it does not abide. Yet it also is not in the absence of time and space, so we say it does not not abide either. Because this name cannot be grasped, we call it absolute stopping and seeing, inconceivable stopping and seeing, birthless stopping and seeing, and also the stopping and seeing of the one great matter. Therefore this great matter is not in contrast to a small matter: just as space is not called vast in reference to a small space, similarly stopping and seeing is not called stopping and seeing in reference to folly and confusion. It is one unique realm of reality that cannot have any opposite; therefore it is called absolute stopping and seeing.

People of the world explain the meaning of *absolute* with various words but after all do not reach absoluteness. Why? Because ordinary feelings motivate conceptualization, speculation and imagination in various ways. They discriminate distinctions of enlightenment and nonenlightenment, mind and nonmind, ordinary and holy. Thus absolute is opposed to nonabsolute, inconceivable is opposed to conceivable; so relativeness continues circularly, and there is nowhere absoluteness can be assigned.

If you get the meaning, you run out of words, and the course of mind also ends: ineffably enlightened in accord with knowledge you have no further subjective discriminations, and you do not speak of enlightenment and nonenlightenment, wise and unwise, mind and nonmind, conceivable and inconceivable, and so on. All kinds of errant conceptions focusing on discriminations of principle are called relative; when true wisdom emerges, it obliterates these oppositions, and the obliteration then is also obliterated, like a stick pushing a fire, eventually burning itself up. This is called absolute. Therefore the *Pure Name Scripture* says, "Phenomena do not await each other, because they do not remain for even an instant." This is the same idea. Being so, the absolute is the sphere of sages, and as such beginners have no part in it; but now if we look at it in terms of the six identities, we see that there is no lack in beginners and no excess in the sphere of sages.

Third is uniting differences. This absolute stopping and seeing is also called inconceivable, and also called great. The major scripture says, "Greatness is called inconceivability." Other scriptures and treatises may refer to stopping as detachment, nondwelling, nonattachment, noncontrivance, or quiescence, and do not distinguish meditation states, rejections, relinquishments, and so on. These are all different names for stopping. Insofar as stopping is absolute, great, and inconceivable, detachment and the rest are all absolute, great, and inconceivable.

Elsewhere, seeing may be called knowledge and vision, clear consciousness, perceptive awareness, wisdom, illumination, insight, and so on. These are all different names for seeing. Insofar as seeing is absolute, great, and inconceivable, knowledge and vision and the rest are all absolute, great, and inconceivable. Why? Wisdom is one, but Buddha expresses it by different names. The same is true of liberation; there are many names for it, just as space is "empty," "immobile," and "unobstructed." We should know that the three attributes are one reality, to which different names are given according to the type of people being addressed. If you hear "absolute," be careful not to be alarmed, and if you hear of uniting differences, be careful not to doubt, or you will hurt yourself. Also, stopping and seeing themselves unite with each other: stopping is also called seeing and also called not stopping; seeing is also called stopping and also called not seeing. This is the same meaning as the preceding analysis of the name.

Fourth is comprehending the three attributes. If the different terms in the scriptures all refer to stopping and seeing, since the names are innumerable the meanings must also be innumerable; why use just three meanings to interpret stopping and seeing? We make this interpretation just to associate them with the three attributes. Since spiritual realities are infinite, why only associate them with the three attributes? The *Great Wisdom* treatise says, "From their first inspiration, bodhisattvas always contemplate nirvana as they practice the Way." The major scripture says, "Buddhas and sentient beings are all stationed in the secret treasury." The secret treasury is nirvana, nirvana is the three attributes, the three attributes are stopping and seeing. Self and others, beginning to end, all can practice and enter; therefore we use these as counterparts.

If we use both terms to comprehend the three attributes, stopping is annihilation, and annihilation leads to liberation; seeing is knowledge, and knowledge leads to wisdom; equal balance of stopping and seeing is relinquishing appearances, and relinquishing appearances leads to the body of reality. Also, stopping is tranquillity, seeing is insight, and by equal balance of tranquillity and insight, one is equanimous; these comprehend the three attributes, as the preceding.

QUESTION: Stopping and seeing are two methods; how can they comprehend the inconceivable three attributes?

ANSWER: They can comprehend by means of inconceivable stopping and seeing, that is all. Also, the *Great Wisdom Scripture* explains eighteen kinds of emptiness to interpret wisdom, and one hundred and eight concentrations to interpret meditation: although these are two interpretations, how can there be no wisdom in meditation or no meditation in wisdom? These are not two, yet two; two, so not two. As not two, they are the body of reality; as two, they are concentration and insight. These three are never apart from each other. Therefore the major scripture says, "Buddha-nature has five names: it may be called heroic progress concentration, or it may be called wisdom, or it may be called neither stopping nor seeing, or it may be called stopping, or it may be called seeing." This is inconceivable stopping and seeing comprehending the inconceivable three attributes.

Furthermore, stopping and seeing each comprehend the three attributes; there is seeing in stopping, there is stopping in seeing. Stopping as cessation is virtue in prohibition and belongs to the category of concentration, thus leading to liberation. Stopping as stationing is virtue in action and belongs to the category of contemplation, thus leading to wisdom. Stopping that is not stopping belongs to noumenon, which leads to the body of reality. The meaning is apparent.

Seeing as piercing is virtue in prohibition, in the category of concentration, leading to liberation. Seeing as perceptive realization is virtue in action, in the category of contemplation, leading to wisdom. Seeing that is not seeing belongs to noumenon, leading to the reality body. Again the meaning is apparent.

Also, stopping and seeing together comprehend the three attributes. Cessational stopping and piercing seeing both get their names from detachment, so they correspond to liberation. Stationary stopping and perceptive realizational seeing both get their names from perceiving knowledge, so they correspond to wisdom. Stopping that is not stopping and seeing that is not seeing are both called the nature of reality, so they correspond to the body of reality.

The three attributes, moreover, correspond to stopping and seeing. Because the three attributes collectively correspond to both terms, the three attributes must also individually correspond to both terms.

As for the collective correspondence of the three attributes, liberation corresponds to stopping, wisdom to seeing, and the reality body to nonstopping and nonseeing.

As for the three attributes individually corresponding to stopping and seeing, liberation, being full liberation, comprises three kinds: expedient purification liberation corresponds to stopping as cessation, complete purification liberation corresponds to stopping as stationing, and the liberation of inherent purity corresponds to nonstopping stopping. Now, wisdom, as full wisdom, comprises three kinds: the wisdom of knowledge of the Path corresponds to piercing seeing; the wisdom of knowledge of all modes of the Path corresponds to perceptive realizational seeing; the wisdom of knowledge of all particulars corresponds to nonseeing seeing. The full reality body also has three kinds: the material body corresponds to one stopping and one seeing; the body of teachings corresponds to one stopping and one seeing, and the body of truth corresponds to one stopping and one seeing. The meaning here is apparent.

If you believe that the three attributes are absolute, great, and inconceivable, once the sense of the correspondence is clear, you should believe that stopping and seeing are absolute, great, and inconceivable. If you believe that nirvana with the three attributes inherent in it is called the secret treasury, you will also believe that the three kinds of stopping fully accomplished, called great silent concentration, are called the secret treasury. You will also believe that the three kinds of seeing, fully accomplished, called great knowledge, are called the secret treasury. You will also believe that nonstopping and nonseeing, with the three attributes inherent, are called the secret treasury. If you believe that the three attributes are not vertical, not horizontal, not lined up, not separate, like the three dots of the Indian *i*, like the three eyes, you will also believe that the three stoppings and three seeings are not vertical, not horizontal, not lined up, not separate.

Nevertheless, the various scriptures, adapting to conditions, just bring up one principle to show one aspect of the meaning. For example, the *Heroic Progress Scripture* just brings up the stopping side of it; stopping includes all the teachings, without lack, and is also called the secret treasury. The *Treatise on the Perfection of Wisdom* and the *Lotus of Truth Scripture* just bring up the seeing side of it; seeing includes all the teachings, without lack. The *Nirvana Scripture* brings up the three principles in full, yet there is no more in it than the others. This is also called the secret treasury. The same is true of stopping and seeing, whether you distinguish them or unite them: there is no more when distinguished, no less when united. Each one is the realm of reality, including all truths; all is the secret treasury. This being so even in the case of partial presentation, how much the more so of complete presentation.

As stopping and seeing correspond to the three attributes in this way, correspondences with the various different terms of detachment, knowledge and insight, and so on, are also like this. Correspondences with other triplexes—three Buddha-natures, three treasures, and so on—are also like this.

QUESTION: How are the meanings of these terms vertical and horizontal, and how are the meanings of these terms not vertical or horizontal?

ANSWER: According to what teachers of the lesser vehicle say, even when wisdom is realized, bondage by results of actions still exists and liberation is incomplete; the body is still mortal and impermanent. One superior and two inferior is likened to a horizontal river or a racing fire. Also it is said that first there is the beatified body, then one attains wisdom, and after that one extinguishes body and knowledge, only then to be liberated. Since here there is the sense of above and below, before and after, it is likened to the vertical three points of the *water* radical in a Chinese character. If one enters concentration as extinction, there is a body but no knowledge. Saints in the formless realm have knowledge but no body. If one enters nirvana without remainder, there is only the liberation of individual pacification. These three are unrelated to each other; if you line them up, they are horizontal, and if you stack them up they are vertical. If you distinguish them, they are different.

According to what teachers of the Great Vehicle say, the body of reality is the true essence; it is originally, inherently there, whether or not there is a Buddha, and is not just now present. The wisdom that is the basis of comprehending this, and liberation free from affliction, both must exist. Across lifetimes, over the ages, they extend throughout purity and defilement. This is the verticality of the meanings of the terms. Also it is said that the three attributes have no sequential priority and are complete in one essence. Insofar as the essence accords with meaning, there are three differences. In sum, the essence is horizontal, while the meanings are vertical, that is all. It is also said that the essence and the meanings are not different, but there is the difference of concealment and revelation. The two not being different still does not escape being horizontal, while the difference of concealment and revelation still does not escape being vertical.

Such are the various interpretations; how can they be reconciled with the scriptures?

Now we make it clear that the three attributes are all inconceivable; how can they be assumed to be vertical? All inconceivable, how can they be assumed to be horizontal? All inconceivable, how can they be assumed to be one? All inconceivable, how can they be assumed to be different? This is interpreting according to the noumenal matrix.

The body is permanent, knowledge complete, annihilation full; all are qualities of Buddha, none is superior or inferior, therefore they are not vertical. The three qualities merge into each other, being the same one realm of reality. Outside the realm of reality, where is there anything else? Therefore they are not vertical. It is possible to define them in various ways, so they are not one, yet they all go back to ultimate truth, so they are not different. This is interpretation according to the practical basis.

Being one yet three, they are not horizontal; being three yet one, they are not vertical. Not three yet three, they are not one; not one yet one, they are not different. This is interpretation according to the usage of terms. This is the real meaning of the metaphor of the triangularly arrayed three dots of the letter *i*, representing not being vertical or horizontal.

QUESTION: What about the meaning of the three attributes [of wisdom, liberation, and reality] and the four attributes [of permanence, bliss, selfhood, and purity]?

ANSWER: Speaking of the three attributes in general, each one is permanent, blissful, self, and pure. The major scripture says, "What Buddhas consider their teacher is reality; because reality is eternal, the Buddhas too are eternal." "Reality" is the body of reality, and "Buddha" is nirvana and liberation; therefore we make a general interpretation. The major scripture says, "By annihilating this body you attain the permanent body; the same is true of sensation, perception, patterning, and consciousness." Thus the body of reality is in every respect permanent, blissful, self, and pure. The same is true of the other two attributes.

Based on individual elements, transforming the physical body produces the reality body, which is permanent and blissful; transforming the consciousness and perception produces wisdom, which is pure; transforming sensation and patterning produces self; and transforming matter produces purity. Thus there are two interpretations, both in general and in particular. Based on the complete teaching, this is the sudden doctrine; based on the separate teaching, this is the gradual doctrine.

Explaining the Essence and Characteristics of Stopping and Seeing

Once you know the overall meaning and comprehend it as hitherto explained, the term is far-reaching, and if you would approach it you should know that the essential principle is very profound. Roughly, we will expose the essence in terms of four notions: (1) doctrine and characteristic, (2) eye and knowledge, (3) sphere, (4) gain and loss.

Now, principle is revealed by doctrine; since doctrines are many, we illustrate them by their characteristics. Since ways into principle are not the same, we show them in terms of eyes and knowledges. There are provisional and real truths, which we reveal by their spheres. Because people are different, we show them in terms of gain and loss.

As for revelation by doctrine and characteristic, the doctrine termed stopping and seeing includes ordinary people and sages; we cannot seek particularized essence by way of an inclusive term; therefore we use characteristics for analysis.

For ordinary people, what is quelled by virtue of prohibition is characteristic of stopping, while what is produced by virtue in action is characteristic of seeing. Also, the four meditations and four immeasurable minds are characteristic of stopping, while the six practices [of the perfections] are characteristic of seeing. As long as all of these have not yet gotten out of birth and death, they are characterized by contamination. Therefore the major scripture says, "None but the Mali Mountains produce sandalwood; there is no true knowledge other than the knowledge of the three vehicles." Therefore this [contaminated stopping and seeing of ordinary people] is not the subject of the present discussion.

As for the two vehicles, with their nine thoughts, ten thoughts, eight rejections, and nine stages of concentration, these are mostly meditations on phenomena, which are on the whole characteristic of stopping. The knowledge of the conditional four truths is characteristic of seeing. Though this stopping and seeing gets out of birth and death, still it is unskillful emancipation. Annihilating form to enter emptiness, this emptiness can also be called stopping, and can also be called neither stopping nor nonstopping, but it cannot be called seeing. Why? Because it is "reducing the body to ashes and extinguishing knowledge," it cannot be called seeing. It is only characterized by analysis of phenomena and noncontamination. It is not the subject of the present discussion.

The stopping that is skillful emancipation is of three kinds. One is stopping by comprehending reality. The second is stopping through expedient adaptation to conditions. The third is stopping by ceasing discrimination of the two extremes.

As for the first, stopping by comprehending reality, all things are born from conditions, and conditions are empty, without basis. Stopping the mind and realizing the source is that whereby one is called tranquil. Knowing that conditions temporarily compound, are illusory productions, and are essentially void is called comprehending. Errant thoughts clinging to objects cease when emptiness is realized; emptiness being reality, this is called stopping by comprehending reality.

As for the second, stopping through expedient adaptation to conditions, if the three vehicles all alike stop affliction and enter truth by the path that has no verbal expression, the truth is no different, but there is the issue of whether afflictions and habits are annihilated or not. If those in the two vehicles comprehend truth, they do not need stopping through expedients, but bodhisattvas who enter the conditional should then use it. Knowing emptiness is not empty, it is called expedient; distinguishing medicines and diseases, it is called adapting to conditions; as the mind rests on the worldly truth, it is called stopping. The scriptural saying "The mind always one, whether in action or repose" can also testify to this idea.

As for the third, stopping by ceasing discrimination of the two extremes, samsara flows, nirvana is secure; both are partial action, partial function, not realizing the Middle Way. Now, if you know the worldly is not worldly, the worldly extreme is quiescent. Also, when you do not grasp the nonworldly, the extreme of voidness is quiescent. This is called stopping by ceasing extremes.

Although I have never seen terms for these three kinds of stopping in scriptures or treatises, I have defined the terms according to meaning, paralleling the three kinds of seeing. The *Treatise on the Perfection of Wisdom* says, "When bodhisattvas create terminology in accord with the teachings of the scriptures, this is called spiritual giving." So there is nothing wrong with creating terms. If you can search out terms from the scriptures, I predict they will accord with these definitions.

On careful examination of these three kinds of stopping, the terms resemble those in the previous analysis of the name, but the characteristics are different. As for the similarities, cessational stopping resembles comprehending reality, stationing stopping resembles expedient adaptation to conditions, and nonstopping stopping resembles ceasing the two extremes. Their characteristics being different refers to the characteristics of the three levels of truth; the former three produce the latter three, and the last one contains the former three. How so?

When stopping by comprehending reality, realizing that conditional phenomena are artificial definitions and are empty, without basis, then the ill of flux ceases; this is the meaning of cessation. Setting the mind on the principle is precisely realizing conditionality; this is the meaning of stationing. This principle is truth, truth is the source, and the source does not call for stopping or not stopping; this is nonstopping stopping. These three meanings together form the characteristics of stopping by comprehending truth.

When stopping by expediency, you perceive the conditional freely, and distraction, confusion, and unknowing cease; this is the meaning of cessation. When you set the mind on the principle of the conditional, like when it says in the *Pure Name Scripture* to enter concentration to observe people's faculties and natures and distinguish remedies and ailments, this is the meaning of stationing. Since the principle of conditionality does not fluctuate, this is nonstopping stopping. Thus the three meanings together form the characteristics of stopping through expedient adaptation to conditions.

When ceasing the two extremes, the characteristics of samsara and nirvana both cease; this is the meaning of cessation. Wisdom entering principle is called dwelling; focusing the mind on the Middle Way is the meaning of stationing. This principle of reality is neither stopping nor not stopping; this is the meaning of nonstopping stopping. Thus these three meanings together form the characteristics of stopping by ceasing the two extremes.

Therefore these are different from the preceding, and also are not the basis of the present discussion.

Next, to explain the characteristics of seeing, there are three kinds of seeing. Going from the conditional into emptiness is called seeing the two truths. Going from emptiness into the conditional is called seeing equality. With these two kinds of seeing as means, you can enter the Middle Way, simultaneously aware of the two truths, each state of mind passing quietly away, spontaneously flowing into the ocean of all-knowledge; this is called seeing the ultimate truth of the Middle Way. These names come from the *Necklace Scripture*.

As for the "two truths," seeing conditionality is a way of clarification to penetrate emptiness; emptiness is understood by clarification. Because subject and object are dealt with together, we call it seeing the two truths. It is like sunlight merging with the sky; you not only see emptiness but also see the conditional, like when the clouds are gone, removing the screen, and above is revealed while below is illuminated. Based on truth, the conditional is revealed, so that this seeing of two truths is realized. Now, understanding truth by way of the conditional, in what sense is this not seeing the two truths?

Also, the mundane is what is broken through, and the real is what is applied. If we go by what is broken through, we should call it seeing the mundane truth, while if we go by what is applied, we should call it seeing the real truth. Because breaking through and application are treated together, we call it seeing the two truths.

There are also three distinctions. In terms of doctrine, there is seeing the two truths according to feelings. In terms of practice, there is seeing the two truths according to knowledge. Although the beginning effort to see does not yet accord with reality, we can speak of seeing the two truths according to doctrine and according to practice.

QUESTION: The first seeing gets its name from breaking through and application together; in the second seeing, there is also breakthrough and application—should it also be called seeing the two truths?

ANSWER: The first one already being named after the two truths, though the next one also breaks through and applies these truths, yet it gets the name of equality from what is superior.

QUESTION: The third seeing also breaks through and applies—why doesn't it get the name from what is superior?

ANSWER: In the first two seeings there is progressive breakthrough and progressive application because there is blockage; in the third seeing there is no blockage, and it just gets its name from what is applied. You cannot make everything into one pattern.

QUESTION: The first two seeings observe both truths, so they should also enter into both truths.

ANSWER: At first we observe conditionality to break through sickness; we observe reality to apply the real: therefore we observe both. One we apply and one we don't apply; therefore we do not enter both.

QUESTION: The real and the middle can be called truths, but how can the mundane, or conventional, be called truth?

ANSWER: The *Scripture on Keeping the Stages* explains two kinds of reality nature: one is the phenomenal reality nature, in that this nature is differentiated; the other is the true reality nature, in that this nature is really true. These are but different names for the two truths. Since both can be called reality nature, why can't they be called truths?

QUESTION: If so, both can be called nirvana.

ANSWER: This is what scripture means when it speaks of a poor man finding a jewel, a monkey getting wine, in that worldly ecstasy is also called nirvana. Thoughtless trance is also the nirvana of the worldly.

QUESTION: Then are both contaminated?

ANSWER: A treatise speaks of "Right insight in the world, right insight beyond the world."

QUESTION: Then are both birthless?

ANSWER: Scripture says, "Different characteristics do not exist in each other."

QUESTION: In penetrating emptiness by way of conditionality, is it necessary to break through the conditional to enter into emptiness?

ANSWER: In all, there must be four possibilities: entering without breaking through, breaking through and entering, breaking through without entering, and neither breaking through nor entering. Ultimately there are thirty-six possibilities, as will be explained later.

As for calling entry from emptiness into the conditional "seeing equality," if one enters emptiness there cannot even be any emptiness; what conditional is there to enter into? You should know that this seeing is for the sake of edifying people. Knowing the real is not the real, we expediently emerge into the conditional; therefore it is called "from emptiness." Distinguishing remedies and ailments without error, it is therefore called entering the conditional. "Equality" is used in contrast to the preceding: the previous seeing, breaking through the disease of conditioning, did not apply the conditional, only the real; breaking through one and not the other is not yet equal. The subsequent seeing breaks through the disease of emptiness and uses conditional phenomena. Since breakthrough and application are balanced, because of the counterbalance of the different phases we call it equal.

Now let us present a simile for this. When the blind get sight for the first time, they see space and form, but even though they see form they cannot differentiate the various types of plants and trees, stems, branches, and foliage, medicinal or poisonous properties. When one enters emptiness from the conditional, following knowledge, one also sees the two truths but cannot use the conditional. After people's eyes are opened, they can see space and form, distinguish varieties, and clearly understand cause and effect; they can recognize coarse and fine medicine and food, and can use them all to benefit others. This is like entering the conditional from emptiness, including both real and mundane, correctly using the conditional for the edification of sentient beings. Therefore it is called entering the conditional, and also called equality.

As for seeing the ultimate truth of the Middle Way, first we see the emptiness of the conditional, which empties samsara, or birth and death; then we see the emptiness of emptiness, which empties nirvana. Stopping the two extremes is called seeing the two emptinesses as the means to harmonize with the Middle Way. This is why it is said that each state of mind passes silently away, flowing into the ocean of all-knowledge.

Also, the first contemplation uses emptiness, the next uses the conditional; this is the method of retaining both. When you enter the Middle Way, you can simultaneously perceive both levels of truth. Therefore scripture says, "If the mind is in concentration, one can know the characteristics of phenomena becoming and passing away in the world." This is wherein lies the meaning of the previous two contemplations being two kinds of technique.

QUESTION: The major scripture says, "Those in whom either concentration or knowledge is preponderant cannot see the Buddha-nature." What does this mean?

ANSWER: Taking the three contemplations in succession, those in the two vehicles and bodhisattvas of the common teaching have a portion of the first contemplation; this is in the category of not seeing Buddha-nature because of having more concentration than knowledge. Bodhisattvas of the separate teaching have a portion of the second contemplation; this is in the category of not seeing Buddha-nature because of having more knowledge than concentration. Using these two contemplations as means to gain entry into the third contemplation, then one perceives Buddha-nature.

QUESTION: Scripture says, "Bodhisattvas in the tenth abode do not see with perfect clarity because they use the eye of wisdom." It is not that they do not see at all; since the final contemplation is the stage of the eye of wisdom, and the second contemplation is the stage of the objective eye, how can you say these two eyes do not see at all?

ANSWER: Those successive eyes are partial to concentration or knowledge and are criticized by Buddha. You cannot say they see. When it says that the eye of wisdom sees, though the name is the same as the wisdom eye of the first contemplation, in reality this is the stage of the tenth abode of the complete teaching. When the three contemplations are present and one enters the inner principles of the truths, this is called abiding, and this abiding is referred to as the eye of wisdom, that is all. This is why the *Lotus Scripture* says, "May we attain supreme purity of the eye of wisdom, like the Buddha."

Thus the perception on the part of the wisdom eye is not perfect. Therefore it is said to be like seeing forms at night, or seeing geese in the sky. But the wisdom eye of the two vehicles does not deserve this name. Therefore the *Lotus Scripture* presents the simile of someone drilling on a high plateau, only seeing dry earth; if he keeps on working, he will see moist earth, eventually reach mud, and after that get water. The dry earth represents the first contemplation, the moist earth represents the second contemplation, the mud represents the third contemplation, and water represents complete seeing all at once.

This also represents the teachings. The Three Baskets

teaching, which does not explain the Middle Way, is like dry earth. The common teaching is like moist earth. The separate teaching is like mud. The complete teaching, explaining the Middle Way, is like water. Being what the first two teachings do not explain, what their two practices do not reach, how can Buddha-nature be perceived by the wisdom eye that is focused only on emptiness? There is no way this eye can see Buddha-nature.

While these three contemplations, as ways of seeing, appear to be the same in name as the previous three kinds of seeing, their meanings and characteristics are different. First let us consider the similarity. The previous "piercing" seeing through falsehoods resembles entering emptiness from the conditional. The previous "perceptive realization" seeing, comprehending noumenon and harmonizing with noumenon, comprehending phenomena and harmonizing with phenomena, resembles the seeing of equality entering into the conditional. The previous "nonseeing" seeing resembles the Middle Way.

As for the differences in characteristics, the previous ones were characterized by one level of truth, while these latter are characterized by three levels of truth. Also, the former three seeings together form the latter three, and the latter three include the former three. How so? As entering emptiness from the conditional breaks through the bedrock of the four basic afflictions, is this not the meaning of "piercing"? The emptiness that is entered into is noumenon, and knowledge can reveal noumenon; this is the meaning of "perceptive realization." This empty noumenon itself is the meaning of "nonseeing seeing." These three meanings together form the characteristics of seeing into emptiness.

Entering the conditional from emptiness also has three meanings. How so? Knowing artificially defined phenomena breaks through the barrier of nonknowing; this is the meaning of "piercing." Awareness of the principles of artificial definition, distinguishing without error, is the meaning of "perceptive realization." The principle of artificial definition, always being so, is the meaning of "nonseeing seeing." These three meanings together form the characteristics of seeing the conditional.

Seeing the Middle Way also has three meanings. Emptying the two extremes is the meaning of "piercing." Correctly entering the Middle Way is the meaning of "perceptive realization." The reality nature of the Middle Way is the meaning of "nonseeing seeing."

This is explaining the characteristics of threefold stopping and threefold seeing based on the Great Vehicle. They are differentiated by meaning and according to characteristics. If we speak of the three kinds of seeing, or contemplation, there are provisional and true, shallow and deep. If we speak of the three knowledges, there are superior and inferior, prior and later. If we speak of three types of people, there are greater and lesser among the various stages. This is gradation, and not what I am going to use now.

As for the characteristics of complete, all-at-once stopping and seeing, when focusing on a truth by stopping, one truth is three truths; fixing stopping by one truth, one stopping is threefold stopping. It is like three characteristics being in one moment of awareness; though it is one moment of awareness, it has three characteristics. Stopping on a truth is also like this; although the truth stopped on is one, yet it is triplex; though the mind that stops is triplex, yet it is one. When observing an object by seeing, one object is three objects; when eliciting seeing by an object, one seeing is triplex seeing. It is like the three eyes on the face of the god Maheshvara; though there are three eyes, it is one face. The same is true of seeing and object: on seeing three, they are one; on awakening one, it is three.

This is inconceivable, not provisional, not true, not superior, not inferior, not before, not after, not lined up, not disparate, not great, not small. Therefore the *Treatise on the Mean* says that things born of conditional relations are empty, are conditional, are in the middle. Also, as the *Diamond Cutter Wisdom Scripture* says, it is like when people have eyes and the sun shines, they can see various forms; if the eye could see alone it would not need the sun, and if there are no forms, even if there are eyes and sun there still is nothing seen. Thus these three elements are simultaneous and inseparable. The eyes represent stopping, the sun represents seeing, and the forms represent objects. These three are simultaneous; at the same time we discuss all three, and in the three we are discussing one. If you see the meaning of this, you understand the characteristic of stopping and seeing of the complete all-at-once teaching.

And this is not limited to three and one, one and three. All the foregoing meanings are in one mind. What is that like? Comprehending that ignorance and delusion are none other than reality in its true aspect is called stopping by comprehending reality. As this true aspect of reality is all-pervasive, whatever the conditions, through all circumstances, peace of mind is undisturbed; this is called stopping by expedient adaptation to conditions. The ceasing of the tranquillity and distraction of nirvana and sam-sara is called stopping by ceasing the two extremes.

Comprehending that all conditional phenomena are empty, emptiness being their true aspect, is called seeing into emptiness. When this emptiness is realized, seeing merges with the Middle Way, and one can know the characteristics of phenomena that become and pass away in the world, perceiving them as they really are; this is called seeing into the conditional. This knowledge of emptiness is identical to the Middle Way, no different; this is called seeing the Middle Way.

When you comprehend reality, the five basic afflictions cease in an instant; this is called the meaning of cessation. The mind focusing on the Middle Way enters knowledge of its true aspect; this is called the meaning of stationing. The nature of the true aspect is the meaning of neither stopping nor not stopping. Also, this one moment of awareness can pierce the five basic afflictions to reach reality, and reality is neither seeing nor not seeing.

These meanings are all in one moment of awareness; there are various distinctions, yet without affecting ultimate reality. Scripture speaks of being able to distinguish the characteristics of things without budging from ultimate truth. Although there are many names, it is all wisdom. Buddha uses many terms; the terms all complete, the meanings are also complete. Relative and absolute, in respect to the essence, are inconceivable; because of inconceivability, there is no obstruction, and because there is no obstruction, there is no lack. This is showing the essence of stopping and seeing by the characteristics of the complete all-at-once teaching.

Second is explaining eyes and knowledges. The

essence is not cognition, not perception, not cause, not effect. It is hard to explain it, harder to show it to others. Although it is not cognition or perception, it can be known and seen by means of eyes and knowledges; though it is not cause or effect, it is revealed by cause and effect. Stopping and seeing are the cause, knowledges and eyes are the result. The cause is the remote basis of revealing the essence, the result is the proximate basis of revealing the essence. The essence is mysterious and subtle and cannot be distinguished; it is in reference to eyes and knowledges that the essence can be interpreted.

Now, first to explain progressive eyes and knowledges, three kinds of stopping and three kinds of seeing being the cause, the three knowledges and three eyes attained are the result. As for the three kinds of stopping, in stopping by comprehending reality, delusion does not arise; by stopping you develop concentration, concentration produces noncontamination; because the wisdom eye opens, you see the ultimate truth and absorption in real truth develops.

Therefore stopping can develop the eye, the eye can apprehend essence, and you realize the essence of reality. By stopping in adaptation to conditions, you emerge into the conditional, blanking out the absolute, and rest the mind on the mundane truth; by this stopping you attain mental command, by which you can distinguish ailments and remedies; the objective eye opens up, breaking through the nescience that obstructs psychic powers; always in concentration, you see the Buddha-lands without duality, and absorption in worldly truth develops. Thus stopping can develop the eye, the eye can see essence, and you realize the essence of the world.

In stopping by ceasing extremes, samsara and nirvana, existence and emptiness, are both annulled. By this stopping one develops concentration on the Middle Way; the enlightened eye opens up, with all-pervasive awareness, and absorption in the Middle Way develops. Thus stopping can develop the eye, the eye can apprehend essence, and one realizes the essence of the Middle Way.

As for the three kinds of seeing, when going from the conditional into emptiness, realizing knowledge of emptiness, you can break through the delusions of views and thoughts and attain universal knowledge. This knowledge can realize essence, realizing the essence of reality. Going from emptiness into the conditional, distinguishing ailments and remedies, various aspects of the teachings, you break through unknowing and develop knowledge of modes of the Path. This knowledge can realize essence, realizing the essence of the world. Stopping the two extremes as means to enter the Middle Way, one can break through ignorance and develop knowledge of all particulars. This knowledge can realize essence, realizing the essence of the Middle Way.

Thus three kinds of stopping and three kinds of seeing collectively develop three eyes and three knowledges, each realizing three essences. This is what is meant by discussing eyes and knowledges by way of revealing essence.

QUESTION: The eyes perceive, the knowledges know; are knowing and perceiving different?

ANSWER: This should be analyzed into four possibilities: knowing and not perceiving, perceiving and not knowing, both knowing and perceiving, neither knowing nor perceiving. Because ordinary people do not realize, they do not perceive; because they do not hear, they do not know. People in the two vehicles realize, so they perceive, and they hear, so they know. The self-enlightened realize, so they perceive, but they do not hear, so they do not know. People on an expedient path hear, so they know, but they have not yet realized, so they do not see.

Furthermore, people who practice on faith have wisdom due to hearing; by this wisdom they develop noncontamination and attain universal knowledge. Because this knowledge is based on hearing, it is called knowing by knowledge. People who practice on the basis of principle attain concentration by meditation; based on concentration they develop noncontamination and attain the eye of wisdom. Because this eye is based on meditation, it is called perceiving by the eye. So knowing and perceiving both realize absolute truth, but they are named according to what they are based on. This distinction is made in reference to the eye of wisdom and universal knowledge; the same pattern applies to the other two eyes and the other two knowledges.

The eyes and knowledges of the unified mind are not like that. If we explain the eyes and knowledges of nonsuccessive stopping and seeing, they are as explained before: stopping itself is seeing, seeing itself is stopping; there is no duality, no distinction. The near route to realizing essence is also like this. The eye itself is knowledge, knowledge itself is the eye; in terms of the eye we speak of perceiving, in terms of knowledge we speak of knowing. Knowing is perceiving, perceiving is knowing. The enlightened eye includes all five eyes, enlightened knowledge includes all three knowledges. All absorptions are contained in the supreme absorption; the heroic progress concentration includes all concentrations. The major scripture says, "If you want to attain knowledge of the Path, knowledge of the modes of the Path, universal knowledge, and knowledge of all particulars, you should learn wisdom."

QUESTION: The treatise explaining this scripture says that the three knowledges are in one mind. How can you say we should learn wisdom if we want to attain knowledge of the Path and the rest?

ANSWER: It is true that the three knowledges are in one mind. This explanation is simply for the purpose of telling people in a way that makes it easy to understand. The *Diamond Cutter Wisdom Scripture* says, "'Does a Buddha have the physical eye?' 'Yes,'" and so on, to "'Does a Buddha have the enlightened eye?' 'Yes.'" Although a Buddha has five eyes, in reality they are not divided up; by one eye having five functions, it is possible to perceive five spheres.

How so? The enlightened eye can also see gross material form as ordinary people do, but can also see more; this is called the physical eye. It can also see subtle form as celestials do, but can also see more; this is called the celestial eye. It perceives the emptiness of gross and subtle forms, as those of the two vehicles see; this is called the wisdom eye. It comprehends artificial designations without error, as bodhisattvas see; this is called the objective eye. It sees the true aspect in all things; this is called the enlightened eye, or the Buddha eye.

You should know that the enlightened eye is completely perceptive, not missing anything. Therefore scripture says, "The five eyes complete, one attains enlightenment, forever to be father and mother of the triplex world." The reason it is solely called the enlightened eye, or the Buddha eye, is that it is like when rivers enter the ocean, the waters lose their names. It is not that the Buddha eye does not have the other four functions.

Enlightened knowledge aware of emptiness, like what those of the two vehicles see, is called universal knowledge. Enlightened knowledge aware of the conditional, like what bodhisattvas see, is called knowledge of the modes of the Path. Enlightened knowledge aware of emptiness, conditionality, and the Middle Way, seeing the true aspect of each, is called knowledge of all particulars. Therefore it is said that the three knowledges are found in one mind.

So we know that the three eyes developed by the three kinds of stopping in one mind perceive the inconceivable three truths; because these perceptions are attained from stopping, they get the name of "eye." The three knowledges developed by three kinds of seeing in one mind know the inconceivable three spheres; because these knowledges are attained from seeing, they get the name of "knowledge."

The truths are different from the spheres only in the same sense that something may be said to be to the right or the left, depending on the point of reference. Perceiving and knowing are only different in name and need not be separately explained. Now, I use spheres to show the knowledges, making the three kinds of seeing easy to understand; I use the truths to label the eyes, making the three kinds of stopping easy to understand. Though I make a threefold explanation, actually it is just one single inconceivable reality. Using the eyes and knowledges of this one reality, we realize the essence of complete all-at-once stopping and seeing.

This interpretation is based on contemplation, not reading scriptures, but as it fortunately accords with the scriptures, I have cited them as evidence to avoid people's rejecting and doubting, and to increase faith.

Third is explaining sphere. If you understand the meanings in the exposition of eyes and knowledges, which reveal the truths and spheres, you do not need explanation of the latter. I add this section for those who do not yet understand.

For practice on faith, it is valuable to learn much, by which discernment to understand the perfect wonder. Practice on principle is based on profound contemplation, by which meditation to perceive the objective sphere. First I will clarify the meaning of explaining the spheres; then I will clarify the distinction and unity of the spheres.

Scripture speaks of exposing the knowledges and perception of Buddhas for sentient beings. If there is no sphere of the Middle Way, knowledge has nothing to know, the eye has nothing to perceive. So we know there must be a sphere for the enlightened Buddha eye. Scripture says, "Whoever in the world has the true celestial eye does not see the Buddha-lands dualistically." If there were no worldly sphere, this eye would not see Buddha-lands. Scripture says, "The celestial eye opens up, the eye of wisdom sees reality." Therefore we know there must be a sphere for the eye of wisdom.

These three truths are inconceivable; having no definite nature, they really cannot be explained. If we explain them for the sake of affinity, there are no more than three senses in which this is done. One is explaining according to mental conditions, which is speaking in accord with others' minds. The second is explaining according to mental conditions and knowledge, which is speaking in accord with one's own and others' minds. The third is explaining according to knowledge, which is speaking in accord with one's own mind.

What is explaining the three truths according to mental conditions? Suppose blind people who do not know what milk is ask others what it looks like and they reply that it is white, like seashells, flour, snow, cranes, and so on. Although they hear these explanations, the blind people still cannot understand the true appearance of milk, and each makes up an interpretation clinging to the notion of seashells, or flour, and so on, competing among themselves with four arguments. Those blinded by the ignorance of ordinary feelings are like this, not knowing that the three truths are differentiated as a compassionate expedient. When you explain the three truths in terms of existence, they are like the blind people who hear that milk is [white] like seashells. When you explain the three truths in terms of emptiness, they are like the blind people who hear that milk is like flour. When you explain the three truths in terms of both emptiness and existence, they are like the blind people who hear that milk is like snow. When you explain the three truths in terms of neither emptiness nor existence, they are like the blind people who hear that milk is like cranes.

Although they hear these explanations, they still do not realize the principle of the truths; these ignorant people after all cannot see the real true characteristics of eternity, bliss, self, and purity. But even though they have not seen, they each cling to emptiness or existence and judge each other based on their own ideas. Thus over time there have been twenty-three schools of interpretation of the two levels of truth, each one with different views, all citing scriptures and treatises, none knowing who is right. If you say they are all right, then the principle is indefinitely multiple; you might say they are all wrong, yet all of them have a textual base. Because of this fact, they cling to their own interpretation and deny others'— although they drink the elixir of immortality, it kills them off.

According to scripture, before they were enlightened Manjushri and Maitreya argued about the two levels of truth, and both fell into hell. In the present age those with ordinary feelings who cling only to one text and stick fast to their bias may be considered able, but I'm afraid they are turning away from the Buddha's message. People like this do not yet recognize the three truths as expounded according to mental conditions. If you know the sense of this, when you hear various explanations you will know the Buddha bent over backward to adapt to faculties and mentalities; since faculties and mentalities are many, the explanations are various. This is explaining the three truths according to others' minds.

As for explaining the three truths according to mental conditions and knowledge, according to mental conditions they are said to be dual, while according to knowledge they are said to be one. If so, we cannot speak of three where there is one. This is explanation for ordinary feelings, which includes all expedient means. Though being one yet three, we wrap them up into only two. In terms of sage knowledge, which includes all genuine realization, though being one yet three, we wrap them up into only one. Because of the interface of mental conditions and knowledge we speak of three truths. It is like people in the stage of conformity, when their senses are purified, who still do not discover reality and see the Middle Way; although they contemplate the three truths, they understand them according to the stage they are in, and only break through the four basic afflictions and the delusions numerous as dust motes and sand grains. Having realized the path of expediency, they just wrap it all up into two truths, absolute and mundane. If they enter the first abode, break through ignorance, and see Buddha-nature, simultaneously aware of the two truths, only then is it called knowledge. This comprehends all three truths, wrapping them all up into the ultimate truth of the Middle Way. Mental conditions and knowledge being discussed together, this is speaking in accord with one's own mind and other's minds.

As for explaining the three truths according to knowledge, from the first abode onward it is not only the Middle Way that is said to be beyond looking and listening; the absolute and mundane are also thus. The three truths are recondite and subtle, only illumined by knowledge, impossible to point out or to think of; all who hear are startled. They are not inside, not outside, not difficult, not easy, not formal, not nonformal, not worldly phenomena, void of external appearances. All propositions of logic are inapplicable; only Buddhas can fully comprehend among themselves. There is no way to talk or think about them; they cannot be pictured or imagined by ordinary sense. Whether one or three, all are inaccessible to feelings. Not even those in the two vehicles can fathom them, much less ordinary people. It is like the true appearance of milk being seen when the eyes are opened; it is a waste of words to describe it to the blind who never will understand. Such an explanation is called explaining the characteristics of the three truths according to knowledge; this is speaking in accord with one's own mind.

Now I will go on to refer to passages of scripture elucidating the two truths, bringing to light the teaching of three truths. When it is said, "Ordinary people can comprehend conditionality and produce contemplative understanding," is this not explaining the mundane according to mental conditions? When it is said, "Comprehending the conditional is empty," is this not explaining the absolute according to mental conditions? This is explaining the two truths according to feelings.

When it is said, "What the minds of ordinary people perceive is called mundane truth, while what the minds of sages perceive is called absolute truth," is this not explaining the two truths according to mental conditions and knowledge? When it is said, "Ordinary people act in the world but do not know the characteristics of the world, and not knowing even the mundane, can hardly know the absolute, so both are not known to ordinary feelings," is this not explaining the two truths according to knowledge?

Since the two truths have three levels of explanation, the three truths can be understood by aligning them with this.

If doubters say that Buddha always expounded the

Teaching based on two truths, and claim that is why there are three levels of the two truths, now I will also demonstrate this. The Buddha always liked the Middle Way; his descent into the world, his birth, his leaving home, his enlightenment, and his demise were all in the middle of the night. "Each form, each scent; nothing is not the Middle Way." If he explained the Middle Way, would he not use three meanings according to circumstances?

Each explanation, moreover, includes the intentions of all four aims. As for the four aims within explanation according to mental conditions, the inner principles of the truths cannot be explained; explanation must be done in words, words must accord with mentality, and the mentalities must be pleased—some are joyful on hearing of the absolute, some are joyful on hearing of the mundane, some are joyful on hearing of the Middle Way. This is using the intent of the aim of the world in explanation according to mental conditions.

People's circumstances and conditions are different; some grow in discipline and wisdom when they hear of nonexistence, some grow in discipline and wisdom when they hear of existence, some grow in discipline and wisdom when they hear of the Middle Way. This is using the intent of the aim of helping the individual in explanation according to mental conditions.

Practitioners break through ills differently; some can break through drowsiness and distraction and so on when they hear the teaching of existence, some can break through drowsiness and distraction and so on when they hear the teaching of nonexistence, and some can break through drowsiness and distraction and so on when they hear the teaching of the Middle Way. This is using the intent of the aim of specific cure in explanation according to mental conditions.

People's entry into enlightenment is not the same; some people's understanding opens up when they hear of nonexistence, some transcend to enlightenment when they hear of existence, some awaken penetration when they hear of the Middle Way. The same is true of the contemplating mind; some become light as clouds or shadows when doing contemplation of existence, some become oblivious of body and mind when doing contemplation of nonexistence, and for some spiritual knowledge becomes clear when they do contemplation of the Middle Way. There are various such dissimilarities; that which belongs to one of the truths but not the other two, that which belongs to two truths but not the other one. Therefore it is said, "When Buddha explains the principle of origination, emancipation is attained in the principle of nonorigination; when Buddha explains the principle of nonorigination, emancipation is attained in the principle of origination." This is using the intent of the aim of ultimate truth.

Thus it is that the *Lotus Scripture* says, "Buddha knows people's various inclinations, various actions, various natures, and various thoughts." This is the four intents. How so? Knowing various inclinations refers to according with the world, knowing various natures refers to producing good people, knowing various actions refers to specific cures, and knowing various thoughts refers to ultimate truth.

Why is "nature" in the province of producing good, and "action" in the province of curing evil? Generally speaking, goodness of nature may be hidden or manifest, and evil in action may also be hidden or manifest. Now let us say, for the sake of argument, that good is obscured and evil is manifest, as in the time before the Buddha appeared in the world, when the good roots of the three vehicles were latent and not manifest. It is therefore said that goodness was then obscure; if the people heard of the three truths, this goodness would emerge, so we know that "various natures" must be in the province of producing good, which can be compared to the aim of helping people.

Furthermore, before Buddha appeared, people's evil actions were manifest, their wrongs, biases, errors and faults evident. In order to break through these evils, Buddha expounded the three truths. So we know "various actions" is in the province of breaking through evil, which can be compared to the aim of specific cures.

As for "various thoughts" referring to ultimate truth, "thoughts" are intellectual elements; when biased, they produce perversion of mind, thought, and view. If people meet teachers who correct this thinking intellect, that produces unperverted mind, thought, and view. Buddha expounded the three truths to correct the intelligence; this is the ultimate truth.

As explaining the three truths according to mental conditions has these four intentions, explaining the three truths according to mental conditions and knowledge and explaining the three truths according to knowledge can also be understood on this pattern. This means three times four, or twelve different ways of explaining the three truths; how can you limit the sages by ordinary sense, saying there is only one kind, clinging contentiously and destroying yourself? If you know that the teachings of the wise are boundless, you will not affirm one while denying another, becoming arrogant and conceited; instead you will be like an intelligent blind person who does not argue about the color of milk.

Diligently practicing the facilitating techniques, conscientious and humble, by the three kinds of stopping realize the three eyes, perceive the three teachings, gain the three knowledges, and know the three truths; with clarity of perception, simultaneous awareness thoroughly awake, like when the clouds are gone and their screen is removed, above is revealed and below is illuminated, then you can judge right and wrong and determine the lion roar.

Second is explanation of division and combination of spheres and knowledges. First I will explain spheres, then knowledges. When the scriptures explain the truths— four, three, two, or one—their divisions and combinations are not the same. Now I shall explain them overall.

The Three Baskets are expedient teachings, only explaining two truths. Bodhisattvas in the beginning and middle focus on absolute reality to subdue the four basic afflictions, causing the fat of afflictions to melt away; they cultivate the practices of the six perfections for three incalculable eons to cause the body of virtues to grow, plant the seeds of the marks and embellishments of Buddhahood for a hundred eons, attain five spiritual powers, acquire the objective eye, perceive mundane truth, distinguish people's faculties and natures, and perform enlightening work by tuning and maturing people. The advanced ones sit on the site of enlightenment and in thirty-four mental stages cut off delusions of thought and views entirely. These thirty-four mental stages are the eight acceptances, eight knowledges, nine nonobstructions, and nine liberations. Also, scripture says there are six hundred births and deaths in a single thought, while the teachers of the *Satyasiddi Treatise* say there are sixty instants in a thought. This just means that one attains the wisdom eye, perceives absolute truth, and attains enlightenment in one thought going from the conditional into emptiness.

In the former case the mundane is observed, in the latter the absolute is observed. The two truths are both clear, but it is different with the disciples; the bodhisattvas just observe the mundane and not the absolute, while those of the two vehicles just observe the absolute and not the mundane. Buddhas can include both, adding the ultimate truth of the Middle Way. The two truths of the Three Baskets are an expedient, and to the two truths is added the Middle Way, another expedient on top of an expedient. Seeing this truth adds the Buddha eye, knowing this truth adds knowledge of all particulars. When divided, there are two; when combined, there are three. These are the characteristics of division and combination of the two truths and three truths in the teaching of the Three Baskets.

Next, to talk about the division and combination of the truths in reference to people of the three vehicles alike cutting off afflictions by the path that has no verbal expression, they are the same in terms of mundane truth, different in terms of absolute truth. The great treatise says there are two kinds of emptiness; emptiness that is just emptiness, and emptiness that is not just emptiness. The major scripture says people of the two vehicles only see emptiness and do not see nonemptiness, whereas the wise do not only see emptiness but can also see nonemptiness. Nonemptiness is great nirvana. The two vehicles' knowledge of only emptiness is like the light of a firefly, whereas the knowledge of bodhisattvas is like the sun. Since the emptinesses are different and the knowledges are different, there is the distinction between two truths, but now they are combined into one absolute truth. Those in the two vehicles understand conditionality and enter into reality; they only enter simple emptiness and cannot enter the conditional from simple emptiness. They do not have the function of teaching others. Bodhisattvas understand conditionality and enter into simple reality, and can enter the conditional from simple emptiness, to teach and emancipate people and purify a Buddha-land. When bodhisattvas of superior faculties understand conditionality and enter reality, first they enter simple emptiness, which is just empty, and then they enter emptiness that is not just empty. Thus they break through ignorance and see Buddha-nature. This is eternally different from the preceding "reality"—how could they be the same one absolute truth?

In ancient times, those who believed in adornment said that the state of Buddhahood is outside the two truths. This one-sided idea is incomplete as doctrine, as we do not thereby know what particular sphere enlightened knowledge is aware of, or what particular delusion it annihilates. If you get the meaning of what I am talking about now, however, this doctrine can be established. Those who believed in unfolding goodness said that the state of Buddhahood is not beyond the two truths; this doctrine is also incomplete, but if you get the meaning of what I am telling about now, the doctrine of not being beyond the two truths can also be established. This is why these have been called the popular two truths since ancient times.

When emptiness that is only empty and emptiness that is not only empty are combined, they are just one ultimate truth; separated, they form two ultimate truths. This is different from the school of the Three Baskets; the third truth in the Three Baskets only has the name of "middle way," without a separate essence—there is no particular perception or knowledge of the Middle Way. The present case is different; the third truth is also called the real or absolute truth, and also called the ultimate truth of the Middle Way; separate essence, perception, and knowledge are there. This is the characteristic of the division and combination of the two truths and three truths in the common teaching.

Next, the explanation of the two truths in the separate teaching is forever distinct from the foregoing. The foregoing mundane and absolute are together the mundane of the separate teaching. Mundane means distinctions of the world; these exist by convention, not in reality. Ordinary people are taken in by the mundane truth, the two vehicles are taken in by the absolute truth. As there is the distinction of existence and nonexistence, this is called mundane convention. The *Glorious Garland Scripture* calls those in the two vehicles "sentient beings distracted by voidness." The major scripture says, "Maitreya and I discussed worldly truth together, and five hundred disciples thought we were talking about real truth." If we talk about two truths, the mundane truth is not analyzed; if we make it three truths, it is analyzed into existence as the mundane and nonexistence as the absolute, in contrast to nonsimple emptiness being the ultimate truth. This is the characteristic of the division and combination in the separate teaching.

Next, the complete teaching just explains one real truth. The major scripture says, "Reality is one truth; expediently it is said to be three." Now, I will also take this as basic. Reality is one truth, expediently it is said to be three: the *Lotus Scripture* says, "I also use different expedients, just to help reveal the ultimate truth." This is the characteristic of the division and combination of two truths, three truths, and one truth in the complete teaching.

Next is an explanation of the division and combination of the four truths. The preceding three truths, two truths, and one truth are all vertical explanations; the four truths are discussed horizontally. There are four kinds of four truths: birth and death, no birth or death, infinite, and uncreate. The birth and death four truths are a horizontal analysis of the two truths of the Three Baskets. The birthless four truths are a horizontal analysis of the two truths of the common teaching. The infinite four truths are a horizontal analysis of the two truths of the separate teaching. The uncreate four truths are a horizontal analysis of the one real truth of the complete teaching.

Now, to combine these fourfold four truths by means of the *Treatise on the Center,* the treatise says, "Phenomena produced by conditions I say are empty. This too is artificial designation; it is also called the Middle Way." "Phenomena produced by conditions" refers to the birth and death four truths, "I say are empty" refers to the birthless four truths, "this too is artificial designation" refers to the birthless four truths, "it is also called the Middle Way" refers to the uncreate four truths.

Second, to explain the division and combination of knowledge, scriptures explain one knowledge, two, three, four, up to eleven or more knowledges. If we speak of three knowledges, they can be used to see the three truths; if there are more or less, what do they see? As for "one knowledge," scripture says, "All Buddhas have the same one body of reality, one mind, one knowledge; they also have the same kinds of power and fearlessness. The unique Buddha-knowledge is knowledge of all particulars; characterized by unity and dispassion, it knows the forms of all kinds of actions." As for this knowledge seeing the three truths, when it is said to be characterized by unity and dispassion, this is seeing the Middle Way; when it is said to know the forms of all kinds of actions, this is simultaneous awareness of the two truths.

"Two knowledges" refers to the provisional and the true. The provisional is universal knowledge and knowledge of modes of the Path, which see the two truths of nonexistence and existence. The true is knowledge of all particulars, which sees the truth of the Middle Way.

"Three knowledges" see the three truths. This is easy to understand, so I will not explain it.

"Four knowledges" is like the great scriptures knowledge of the Path, knowledge of modes of the Path, universal knowledge, and knowledge of all particulars. Commentaries interpret these in many ways. Some say in cause there is only essential principle, and this is called knowledge of the Path and knowledge of modes of the

Path, while in effect principle and actuality are both fulfilled, and this is called universal knowledge and knowledge of all particulars.

Some say that knowledge of the Path and knowledge of modes of the Path are spoken of because of the provisional and true within cause; entry into emptiness is considered true knowledge, while entry into the conditional is considered provisional knowledge. Some say universal knowledge and knowledge of all particulars are spoken of because of the provisional and the true in effect; directly focusing on the Middle Way they call universal knowledge, while simultaneous awareness of the two truths they call knowledge of all particulars. Some say these four knowledges refer to the total and the particular in cause and the total and the particular in effect. Some say knowledge of the Path and knowledge of modes of the Path elucidate provisional and true simply, while universal knowledge and knowledge of all particulars elucidate provisional and true in a complex way. Thus the four knowledges are interpreted in various ways; but the four knowledges just perceive the three truths. If there are elucidations of five truths, or six, seven, eight, nine, ad infinitum, as long as you understand this meaning you can interpret them so as to fit them into the three truths.

As for the eleven knowledges, worldly knowledge and knowledge of others' minds both perceive the mundane truth; eight knowledges see the absolute truth; and true knowledge sees the Middle Way.

This is called knowledge having division and combination without altering the three truths.

Furthermore, when knowledge and truths are both divided up, whether they be many or few they inherently include each other. For example, in the case of the three truths there are three knowledges, for the two truths there are two knowledges. The meaning of this is easily understood. In the case that knowledges and truths are both undivided, based on one truth and one knowledge, there is no more and no less. This too is easily understood. Whether knowledges are divided up or combined, ultimately it is true knowledge that is able to reveal true essence.

Next, to explain in terms of truths and knowledges together, the absolute truth of the Three Baskets awakens one eye and one knowledge; the mundane truth awakens one eye and one knowledge; the two truths together awaken one eye and one knowledge. The wisdom eye and universal knowledge relate to absolute truth, the objective eye and knowledge of modes of the Path relate to the mundane truth, and the Buddha eye and knowledge of all particulars relate to both absolute and mundane truths. It cannot be said that both truths are simultaneously illumined together, only that they are illumined in succession.

In the common teaching, absolute truth awakens two eyes and two knowledges, while the mundane truth awakens one eye and one knowledge. Universal knowledge and knowledge of all particulars both relate to absolute truth, while knowledge of modes of the path relate to mundane truth.

If we make the separate link with the common, the mundane truth awakens one eye and one knowledge, the absolute truth awakens one eye and one knowledge; further analyzing the absolute to produce the Middle Way awakens one eye and one knowledge. Each of the three truths in the separate teaching awakens one eye and one knowledge. The knowledge relating to the truths is also like this. If we construe two truths according to the separate teaching, the emptiness within the mundane awakens one eye and one knowledge, the existence within the mundane awakens one eye and one knowledge, and the absolute truth awakens one eye and one knowledge. The knowledges relating to the truths are also like this.

As for the complete teaching, the one real truth awakens three eyes and three knowledges. The knowledges relating to the truth are also like this.

QUESTION: How can the separate link with the common?

ANSWER: First, the twofold contemplation of emptiness and conditionality breaks through delusions about the absolute and the mundane; only then can one hear about the Middle Way. Then one must cultivate contemplation to break through ignorance, whereby one will be able to attain Buddhahood. Buddhahood is the result, the previous two contemplations are the cause; therefore we speak of the separate linking with the common. The result does not link with the cause in three incalculable eons and one hundred eons of cultivating the marks of Buddhahood, so it does not link with the Three Baskets. This result is not linked with the causes in the ten stages, so it does not link with the separate teaching. This result does not link with the annihilation of ignorance in the ten abodes, so it does not link with the complete teaching. It is only possible to link the separate to the common.

Fourth, to explain gain and loss, "loss" is conceptualization, "gain" is nonconceptualization. If you say, "Knowledge arises from mind and naturally illumines objects like a lamp shining on things; as these things exist whether or not they have been illuminated, objects are naturally so whether or not you observe them," then the truths and knowledges do not depend on one another. If you say, "Knowledge is not of itself knowledge, it is knowledge because of objects; objects are not themselves objects, they are objects because of knowledge—it is like long and short being relative to each other," then they exist dependent on one another. If you say, "Objects are not of themselves objects, nor are they objects because of knowledge; objects and knowledge are such because of causes and conditions," this is naming them as a combination. If you deny all three of these explanations and say that objects and knowledge just spontaneously exist as such, then these are objects and knowledge without cause. These four interpretations are all flawed, because they contain four kinds of clinging, and so have dependency. When there is dependency, one is judgmental; then there is like and dislike, which produce all afflictions. Because afflictions have arisen, falsification and contention arise. Because of contention one acts, speaks, and thinks compulsively, thereby revolving in an ocean of misery with no prospect of liberation.

You should know that the four clingings are the root of birth and death; that is why Nagarjuna cut them down. Things are not born of themselves, so how can there be objects and knowledge of themselves? Things are not born from others, so how can there be objects and knowledge depending on each other? There is no collective birth, so how can there be conditional objects and knowledge? There is no birth without cause, so how can there be spontaneously existing objects and knowledge? If you cling to these four views, folly and delusion will be rife; how can this be called knowledge?

Now we have refuted four natures [self-caused, other-caused, collectively caused, causeless] by pointing out that things are not born of themselves, and so on. The four natures refuted, there is no dependence, and so no conditioned action and suffering and so on; the pure mind always unified, then one can perceive wisdom. In terms of this doctrine, suffering and its accumulation in self-existent objects and knowledge does not arise; this means the birth of birth cannot be said. Suffering and its accumulation in causeless objects and knowledge does not arise; this means the nonbirth of nonbirth cannot be said. The path of verbal expression ended, the sphere of mental rumination is obliterated.

But even though these cannot be explained, yet they can still be explained under the conditions of the four aims. One may speak of self-born objects and knowledge, and so on, including causeless objects and knowledge; but though one makes these four explanations, clinging to the four natures is forever destroyed, as above; there are only names, and names have no essence. Essenceless names neither abide nor do not abide; this is inconceivable. Therefore when the *Golden Light Scripture* says, "The objects of inconceivable knowledge, inconceivable knowledge perceives," this is what it means.

If you undermine the objects and knowledges of four natures, this is termed real wisdom; if you explain the four objects and knowledges according to the audience by way of the four aims, this is termed provisional wisdom. For ordinary people, these four objects and knowledges are loss in both senses; for those in the two vehicles, there is gain in one sense and loss in one sense; for bodhisattvas there is gain in both senses. How so? For ordinary people, their own practice while affirming any of the four natures is loss, and to teach others without the four aims in loss. For those in the two vehicles, their own practice of refuting the four natures and penetrating ultimate truth is gain, while not teaching or liberating others is loss. Bodhisattvas achieve both, so both are gain.

Both losses of ordinary people, furthermore, are conceivable, and the one gain and one loss of the two vehicles are conceivable; but the two gains of bodhisattvas are both inconceivable. This is an explanation of gain and loss in terms of the common teaching. As the separate teaching looks on the common teaching, two gains in the common teaching are both conceivable, while the two gains in the separate teaching are both inconceivable. As the complete teaching looks upon the separate teaching, both gains in the way of teaching of separate teaching are conceivable. Why? According to the expedient method of teaching, it may be said that ignorance produces all things, or that reality nature produces all things, or that conditional practice reveals real practice, or that the real appears on its own; if you cling to any of these, it produces the error of intrinsic nature and falls into conceivability. If you realize the Path, it is inconceivable. In the complete teaching, however, both the way of teaching and the realization of the path are inconceivable. Why? The ultimate principle has no explanation; the four explanations made to relate to specific audiences only have artificial designations, and the terms of artificial designations are birthless; therefore teaching and realization are both inconceivable. Because there is no conceptualization, no thought, there is no dependence, no false description, no compulsive action. Because there is no compulsive action, there is no birth and death. This is called gain in one's own practice. Attaining the true essence, one can guide people with inexplicable explanation, enabling them to leave birth and death and realize the true essence. This is self and others both attaining the essence.

Explaining Inclusion of All Things

Doubters say the terms *stopping* and *seeing* are general and do not completely include all things. Now I deny this. Stopping and seeing hold the totality, taking in all things. How so? Stopping can silence all things, like when using moxibustion for sickness; if you find the right point, all ills will clear up. Seeing can clarify principle, like the king of jewels by which all treasures can be obtained. Thus stopping and seeing fulfill all elements of Buddhism. The major scripture on perfection of wisdom has one hundred twenty articles, extending to all things, for which it says one must learn wisdom. Wisdom is just the knowledge of seeing; the knowledge of seeing already embraces all things. Also, stopping is the king concentration; all concentrations enter into it.

Now, to further discuss inclusion of all things more extensively, I construe six meanings: (1) including all truths, (2) including all delusions, (3) including all knowledge, (4) including all practices, (5) including all stages, (6) including all teachings. As for the order of these six, whether or not there is a Buddha, the essence of truth always exists; by missing truth one produces the delusions of samsara, birth and death. By seeing in accord with truth we speak of knowledge; by virtue of understanding we establish practices; by practices we realize stages; by virtue of fulfillment of the stages we teach others. Phenomena and principles, understanding and action, cause and effect, self and others; such successive elements are all included in stopping and seeing.

First is embracing all truths by three kinds of stopping and three kinds of seeing. The truths are as analyzed and synthesized above, with differences of partiality and completeness. Outside the provisional and the true, there are no separate truths; there is no sandalwood elsewhere than Mali Mountain. If there were any other, it would be falsehood. Once we have revealed the essence by stopping and seeing, they contain all truths.

Second is stopping and seeing taking in all delusions. By missing truths one produces the delusions of birth and death. Delusion is ignorance. If you miss provisional truth, there is combined ignorance and solitary ignorance inside the world. That which is conjoined with compulsions of views and thoughts is called combined, while that which is not conjoined is called solitary. Because of not knowing the fact, one arouses greed; not knowing is ignorance, arousing greed is action, greed is consciousness. Consciousness arises together with four other clusters; this is name and form. Form stirs the faculties; this is the six senses. What the six senses attach to is contact. Contact going along with sense data is sensation. Sensation's pleasure constitutes craving. Ties that spring up together with craving constitute grasping. Creating compulsive action toward the future life constitutes becoming. The origination of the future cluster constitutes birth. The ripening of the clusters is aging. Relinquishing the clusters is death. The twelve links of this cycle are causes and effects of each other. Afflictions lead to compulsive action, compulsive action leads to suffering, suffering leads to affliction; thus these are called the three courses.

In scriptures this twelvefold process is called twelve links or the twelvefold wheel or cycle. Because it binds endlessly it is called a wheel or cycle; because of the separation of past, present, and future it is called individual birth and death. It covers up the truth so that one does not attain liberation. This is the ailment. When we have explained the ailment, we know the remedy. The remedy here is stopping and seeing going from the conditional into emptiness. When we see the remedy, we know the ailment; so this delusion is taken in by stopping and seeing entering emptiness.

If you miss the absolute truth, there is combined ignorance and solitary ignorance beyond the world. Why? Although you cut off combined and solitary ignorance inside the world, yet there is still habit energy. The habit energy in the lesser vehicle is not active compulsion; in the true explanation of the great vehicle, habit energy is particularized delusion—this is ignorance beyond the world. Therefore the *Precious Lineage Treatise* says, "Although people in the two lesser vehicles have the specific cures of contemplation of impermanence, misery, emptiness, and selflessness, in respect to the reality body of Buddha these are still inversions." Inversion is ignorance in isolation. The action of uncontaminated knowledge being "action," there are three kinds of mentally produced bodies, or five kinds of mentally produced bodies; the mind is consciousness, the body is name and form, the six senses, contact, and sensation. The artifice of the subtle delusions of ignorance not being ultimately extinguished is craving and grasping. Defilement by afflictions, actions, and birth not being ultimately ended is becoming. Movement is the three kinds of mental causes; the transformations of the result are aging and death. In all, these twelve are four kinds of obstruction in the realm of noncontamination; that is, conditioning, appearances, becoming, and decay. Conditioning is the course of affliction, appearances are the course of action, becoming and decay are the course of suffering. So we know there are the twelve causal conditions beyond the world. Why? All below Buddhahood have ignorance. Ignorance fertilizes action, and once action has been fostered, how can there be no suffering? Although this twelve-link wheel does not regress and degenerate, nevertheless it circles from ignorance to aging and death, circles from aging and death to ignorance. Truth is screened by this delusion. This delusion is cured by seeing into conditionality and seeing into the Middle Way.

Let us consider this further. Why? There are many varieties of the three kinds of mentally produced body. In the case of those of the two vehicles and bodhisattvas of the common teaching, using analysis and comprehension they first annihilate delusion within the world but have not yet cultivated the conditional and the Middle Way; they are born beyond the world, and their delusions beyond the world are completely unconquered, so their faculties are dull. If they then cultivate seeing, they will need to practice gradually for ages and learn innumerable enlightened teachings, and first break through the delusions as numerous as particles of dust and sand. Even if these delusions do not influence becoming, they can obstruct the path of edification, so they must be extinguished first. To extinguish these delusions, stopping is the method of tuning the mind to subdue delusions beyond the world; then they can go on to cut off the three courses of afflictions, compulsive action, and suffering, so that combined and solitary ignorance, branch and root, are all gone.

So we know that seeing conditionality does indeed take in the delusions numerous as particles of dust and sand, and also takes in ignorance. In the case of people of the separate and complete teachings, common delusion is first ended, then particular delusions are subdued. Those born in that realm have sharp spiritual faculties; they only practice the Middle Way to quell the three courses. From the first stage to the last stage the three courses exist in each stage; ignorance dies out bit by bit in each stage, compulsive action dies out, and suffering dies out. When combined ignorance disappears in each stage, so does solitary ignorance. Although there is knowledge in each stage, the knowledge is mixed with ignorance. Being mixed, it is also called the barrier of knowledge, because it inhibits higher knowledge.

Only in the mind of a Buddha is there no ignorance, so

the course of afflictions ends. Because the course of afflictions ends, compulsive action ends. Because compulsive action ends, suffering ends. The ultimate end of the three courses is only in Buddhas. Therefore seeing the Middle Way takes in delusions within and beyond the world.

Fourth is stopping and seeing including all practices. The aforementioned knowledge is understanding; understanding without practical action never gets anywhere. There are two kinds of practice: practice of wisdom and practice of action. In terms of wisdom practice and action practice in the Three Baskets, up to wisdom practice and action practice in the complete teaching, wisdom practice is the main practice, while action practice is assisting practice. Seeing can break through afflictions, yet needs the power of stopping to assist correct knowledge and perception. The main and assisting practices operate following knowledge, just as the feet follow the eyes.

In the Three Baskets, analytic contemplation of impermanence is wisdom practice; contemplation of impurity, kindness, and so on, is action practice. These two practices, following analytic knowledge, enter emptiness.

In the common teaching, comprehending that phenomena are like illusory phantasms is wisdom practice; breath counting, the points of mindfulness, and stopping and seeing focusing on phenomena and going through all things are action practice. These two practices, following knowledge of modes of the path, enter the conditional.

In the Middle Way, focusing on reality, one single path pure and clear, is wisdom practice. Going through all aspects of the teaching—"the perfections are all the Great Vehicle," "the twelve causal conditions are identical to the Buddha-nature," "the points of mindfulness are identical to sitting on the site of enlightenment," and so on—this is action practice. These two practices, following knowledge of the Middle Way, enter reality.

Furthermore, in the basic four meditations, concentration and knowledge are equal, so they are contained in both stopping and seeing. In the realm of desire there is little concentration, more knowledge, so it is taken in by seeing. The four empty concentrations, in which concentration preponderates over knowledge, are in stopping.

Of the four immeasurable minds, the first three [kindness, compassion, joy] are included in seeing; the mind of equanimity is included in stopping.

The nine thoughts, the eight recollections, and the ten thoughts are in seeing.

Of the eight rejections, the first three are in seeing, the last five in stopping.

The nine-step concentration, the lion-leap meditation, and the transcending meditation are in stopping.

The four points of mindfulness are in the sphere of intellectual seeing; if we explain them as stopping on four ideas, attentively remembering impurity, and so on, this is in stopping, but seeing is after all principal.

The four right efforts, to perfect the points of mindfulness, are in one sense in seeing; but the two efforts to stop and prevent bad states are in stopping, while the two efforts to produce and foster good states are in seeing.

In the four bases of spiritual powers, concentration is achieved through four causal conditions; named after the effects, they are in the province of stopping.

Of the five faculties, the three faculties of faith, vigor,

and awareness are in seeing, while remembering and concentration are in stopping. Faith and remembering also belong to both stopping and seeing. The five powers are also like this.

Of the seven elements of enlightenment, discernment, joy, and vigor are in seeing, while ease, equanimity, and concentration are in stopping; mindfulness is in both.

Of the eightfold right path, right insight and right thinking are in seeing. Right action, right speech, and right livelihood, being in the province of discipline, are in stopping. Right mindfulness, right concentration, and right effort are in stopping.

Three of the four truths, being conditioned, belong to seeing. The truth of extinction, being unconditioned, belongs to stopping.

The sixteen practices are all seeing.

The four universal vows are produced based on the four truths, and are like them.

Of the eighteen unique qualities of Buddhas, thought, word and deed according with knowledge and wisdom are in seeing. Impeccability of thought, word, and deed belongs to stopping. Knowledge of past, present, and future belongs to seeing. The rest are obvious.

Of the four fearlessnesses, the fearlessness that comes from universal knowledge belongs to seeing, the fearlessness that comes from extinction of contaminations is in stopping, fearlessness in explaining the Path to end suffering is in seeing, and fearlessness in explaining all obstacles to the Path is in stopping.

The three doors of concentration are in stopping; the three doors of liberation are in seeing.

Of the six perfections, the first three are virtues, in the province of stopping; the last three are knowledge, in the province of seeing. Also, the first five, as virtues, belong to stopping, while insight belongs to seeing. All six perfections, furthermore, as adornments of virtue, belong to stopping.

The nine kinds of great meditation and one hundred eight concentrations all belong to stopping. The eighteen voids, ten similitudes, and five hundred mental controls all belong to seeing.

Thus all practices of insight and action are subsumed in stopping and seeing. You should know that the terms *stopping* and *seeing* are general, while the range of meanings included is wide.

Fifth is stopping and seeing including all stages. If we say the first stage is itself the second stage, the second stage itself the third—in quiescent thusness what successive stages are there?—then there are no successive stages. And yet, here and there in the Great Vehicle scriptures they explain all stages and grades. Indeed, by true knowledge of nonexistence of origin and destruction, where there is nothing to grasp, it is possible to quell afflictions, compulsive actions, and suffering; if these three courses are purged, within the uncreate reality there are still distinctions, so what objection is there to successive stages?

In the case of the three courses being cut off by two approaches, existence and nonexistence, analyzing phenomena to penetrate into emptiness, like the different stages of seven ranks of sages and seven ranks of saints, the four fruits of purification explained in the Abhidharma, and the twenty-seven ranks of sages and saints explained in the *Satyasiddhi Treatise*—all these, up to the stage of the approach of neither existence nor nonexistence, are subsumed in seeing emptiness by analysis.

If the three courses are cut off by entering emptiness through four approaches [being, nonbeing, both, neither] by comprehending things, like the common stages of the three vehicles explained in the major scripture on transcendent wisdom, the stage of dry wisdom up to the eighth stage of bodhisattvahood are alike contained in stopping and seeing entering emptiness.

As for going from emptiness into the conditional, cultivating practice through the realm of differentiation, those who do not realize the intent attain the grade of subduing delusion in thirty mental stages; this is subsumed under the twofold seeing of emptiness and the conditional. Those who realize the intent can break through the three courses and attain the tenth stage of bodhisattvahood; this is in the province of the third seeing [of the Middle Way]. Alternatively, it might be subsumed entirely by seeing the conditional, this applying to existence, nonexistence, both, and neither as well.

In the complete teaching, the phenomena of faith, understanding, and action are themselves reality; from the stage of contemplative practice, one enters the stage of conformity, then goes on to break through ignorance to reveal and realize the knowledge and vision of Buddhahood. In all there are forty-two stages, alike riding the precious vehicle directly to the site of enlightenment. The *Nirvana Scripture* speaks of the moonlight increasing up until the fifteenth of each lunar month as representing the quality of knowledge, and the gradual waning of the moonlight from the sixteenth on as representing the quality of annihilation. Fourteen insights, furthermore, are like the stage of cause, and the fifteenth is like ineffable enlightenment, the stage of result. All of these are subsumed by seeing; this applies to all four approaches.

QUESTION: The Great Vehicle doesn't expound stages; what is contained in stopping and seeing?

ANSWER: The scriptures and treatises of the Great Vehicle all expound stages. Fearing stages, you go into nonexistence of stages, unable to escape bondage by negativity. Words being inherently unconnected to reality, they are at liberty to explain stages, yet it is the same as there being no stages.

The *Treatise on the Middle Way* says, "If, as false teachers do, you deny cause and effect, there is no interconnection of present and future; if you deny transmundane cause and effect, there are no Three Treasures, Four Truths, or Four Fruits of Purification." What Three Treasures are negated? As long as views are not extinguished, there are no Three Treasures, Four Truths, or Four Fruits as in the Three Baskets teaching. Then one does not even attain the fruit of the path of unskillful emancipation; so how could there be the subsequent three levels of the Three Treasures, Four Truths, and Four Fruits? This refutes the false teachers' total negation of the four levels of the Three Treasures, Four Truths, and Four Fruits. If you deny unskillful emancipation, there are only the Three Treasures, Four Truths, and Four Fruits of the Three Baskets, and none of the three subsequent levels of fruits of the path.

According to my refutation, there are Three Treasures,

Four Truths, and Four Fruits of purifying practice. Why? If you break through the afflictions, conditional actions, and suffering within the world by analysis, then there are the Three Treasures, Four Truths, and Four Fruits as in the Three Baskets. If you break through by comprehension, there are the other three levels of Three Treasures, Four Truths, and Four Fruits. By curing lingering in the lesser vehicles and refuting false doctrines, getting rid of extreme views, the true Three Treasures and Four Truths are established; how can it be said they do not exist?

But the affirmation or negation of stages is not understood except by realization. For now just believe in the teaching; if there is teaching, stages are clear. If there is no teaching, there is voidness like the clarity of space. No doctrine is the doctrine of bodhisattvas; even when partitioning emptiness to expound stages, the stages cannot be grasped. This should not be a cause for argument.

We can also find the sense of stages in the four lines of the earlier quoted verse of the *Treatise on the Middle Way:* "Things produced by conditions / I say are empty" breaks through afflictions, conditioned action, and suffering; then there is the knowledge and detachment of stream enterers. This is bodhisattvas' acceptance of nonorigination. The first six stages are on a par with the two vehicles, the seventh stage is expedient means, the tenth stage is like Buddhahood. These stages are clear of themselves; how can you say they do not exist? The verse goes on to say, "This too I call artificial description," referring to gradual successive destruction of the three courses beyond the world, in which there are forty-two stages of sagehood and sainthood; how can you say there are none?

The last line of the verse, "It is also called the Middle Way," refers to the complete destruction of the five basic afflictions, which involves the stages of the six identities; how can you say there are none? In only four lines, all stages are included; all stages do not go beyond the four lines, and the four lines do not go beyond stopping and seeing. Therefore we say stopping and seeing include all stages.

Sixth is including all teachings. As explanatory commentary says, the mind can make terms for all things—without mind there would be no names. You should note that all worldly and trunsmundane terms come from mind. If the mind goes wrong and follows the flow of ignorance, then all kinds of wrong teachings based on false views arise. There are also good teachings that arise—worldly knowledge, without the path to liberation. All these arise from mind.

What about teachings in transmundane terms all coming from mind? Sthiramati's *Precious Lineage Treatise* says, "There is a vast volume of scripture, large as a billion-world universe, recording the phenomena of the universe, to the extent of all the galaxies, planetary systems, and worlds, recording all these things in a single atom; and as this is so of one atom, so it is of all atoms. One person comes into the world, sees this great scripture with the clairvoyant eye, and thinks, 'Why is this scripture inside an atom, and not benefiting all living beings?' So that person uses appropriate means to break the scripture out for the benefit of others. The scripture of the unhindered knowledge of those who realize suchness is all there within the bodies of living beings, yet delusion obscures it, so they don't believe in it or see it. Buddha teaches people to practice the eightfold holy path, to break through all falsehood and see that their own knowledge is equal to the enlightened who realize suchness."

This presents a simile in terms of an atom, in connection with existence; there are also similes made in terms of emptiness. The *Treatise on Awakening the Aspiration for Enlightenment* says, "It is as if someone sees the teaching of Buddha dying out, and so writes the whole canon of Buddha's teaching in the sky; nobody knows about it, until after a long time someone traveling in the sky sees the canon and regrets that people don't know about it, or even see it. So then that person copies the canon and shows it to people to guide them." What is copying the canon? It means to get people to practice the eightfold right path to break through falsehood, and so on.

There are many kinds of practice. If you practice the eightfold right path observing the inconstancy of the conditioned arousal and subsiding of mental states, this is copying out the canon of the Three Baskets. If you practice the eightfold right path observing the emptiness of mental conditions, this is copying out the canon of the common teaching. If you observe that there are innumerable kinds of discrimination and judgment in the mind, which ordinary people and those on the two vehicles cannot fathom, this is practicing the infinite eightfold right path, copying out the canon of the separate teaching. If you see mind itself is Buddha-nature and practice the eightfold right path completely, this is copying out the canon of the Middle Way.

This makes it clear that all teachings come from mind.

Mind is the great vehicle, mind is the Buddha-nature; by yourself you see that your own knowledge is equal to those who arrive at suchness.

Furthermore, observing the mind as being conditional and also in the middle takes in the *Flower Ornament Scripture*. Observing the arising and passing away of conditional states in the mind takes in the teaching of the four Agamas in the Three Baskets, the scriptures likened to milk. Observing the mind as being empty takes in the common *Wisdom* scriptures, likened to cream. Fully observing that conditioned states in the mind are empty, are conditional, and are in the middle takes in the *Universally Equal* scriptures, likened to raw curd. Just using the identity of emptiness, conditionality, and the Middle Way takes in the major *Wisdom* scripture, likened to ripe cheese. To observe the mind on the basis of identity with the Middle Way takes in the straightforward *Lotus Scripture,* likened to ghee, which reveals the great matter of the knowledge and vision of Buddhas. To observe the mind on the basis of the mutual identity of the four propositions takes in the *Nirvana Scripture,* likened to ghee, in which all see the Buddha-nature.

If you contemplate the conditional, moreover, and view conditions as identical to Buddha-nature, and Buddha-nature as being Buddha, this is called killing the person in milk. If you contemplate analytic emptiness and view analytic emptiness as being Buddha-nature, and Buddha-nature as being Buddha, this is called killing the person in cream. If you contemplate intrinsic emptiness and view intrinsic emptiness as Buddha-nature, this is called kiling the person with raw curd. If you contemplate temporal convention and view temporal convention as Buddha-nature, this is killing the person with ripe cheese. If you contemplate the intrinsic mean and view the intrinsic mean as Buddha-nature, this is called killing the person with ghee. Now, what is meant by "killing the person" in all these cases is that the two kinds of death [individual and transformational] have been ended, and the three courses [of affliction, compulsive action, and suffering] are purged. This is called killing the person. This is stopping and seeing containing the unfixed teaching.

The summary inclusion of all teachings in stopping and seeing is as above. As for the matter of extensive inclusion, in fact the teachings of all the scriptures are included in stopping and seeing.

The mind containing all teachings, furthermore, has two general meanings. One meaning is that all the teachings are in the minds of all sentient beings; the Buddha clearly perceives their states of mind and teachings with consideration for their minds, so infinite teachings emerge from mind. The other meaning is that Buddha had practiced gradual and all-at-once observation of mind in the past, both partial and complete; he spoke to people based on this mental observation, teaching disciples to learn how the enlightened one broke open an atom to produce a scripture, and wrote the canon in the sky. Thus did there come to be all the books of scripture. All of this is contained in three kinds of stopping and seeing.

The foregoing six senses of inclusion are to be understood in order. Now, to simply include all things in one thing, one truth includes all truths, all delusions, all knowledges, all practices, all stages, and all teachings; and one delusion includes all truths, knowledges, practices, stages, and teachings; and one knowledge includes all truths, delusions, practices, stages, and teachings; and one practice includes all truths, delusions, knowledges, practices, stages, and teachings; and one stage includes all truths, delusions, knowledges, practices, and teachings; and one teaching includes all truths, delusions, knowledges, practices, and stages.

GLOSSARY

of Technical Terms

Abhidharma Analytic treatises written by early Buddhist masters elucidating the terminology and metaphysics of the sermons of Buddha.

abode of treasure A symbol of omni-science, or all-knowledge, the ultimate goal of complete development envisioned by Mahayana Buddhism, in which all dharmas, or phenomena, are regarded as Dharma, or Buddhist teaching.

accords Principles of appropriately adapted teaching: according to inclinations, according to situations, according to appropriate remedy, according to beneficial meaning.

afflictions Defects of character and mentality that drain the psyche and interfere with correct awakening. The six major afflictions defined in Buddhist literature are greed, hatred, folly, conceit, doubt, opinionation. The "four basic afflictions" are egotistic folly, egotistic opinion, egotistic pride, and egotistic attachment. The "five basic afflictions" are localized views, attachment to desire, attachment to forms, attachment to being, and ignorance.

Agama scriptures Discourses of Buddha belonging to the so-called Small Vehicle teaching, or what Chih-i classifies as the Three Baskets teaching.

aims The four aims, or ends (*siddhanta*), of the teaching: the aim of the world, for objective understanding; the aim of helping people, for personal development; the aim of curing, for remedying specific problems; and the aim of ultimate truth, for realization of the absolute.

Ajatashatru A king who killed his father and imprisoned his mother, thus representing an archetype of evil. While imprisoned, the king's mother was the initial recipient, in a vision, of the teaching of the scripture known as *Visualization of Infinite Life,* one of the main texts of Pure Land Buddhism.

Amitabha The Buddha of Infinite Light, archetype of cosmic compassion; the Buddha of the Western Pure Land of Bliss, object of devotion of Pure Land Buddhists.

Angulimalya An aberrant cultist of Gautama Buddha's time, whose name comes from his garland of human finger bones, made from bones of people he himself had sacrificed to his belief. Angulimalya was liberated from his delusions when he met the Buddha; his name is cited in scripture as a symbol of aberration and evil being yet susceptible to redemption.

arhat Conventionally, a Buddhist "saint" of the lesser vehicle of listeners; arhats have attained individual release and enjoy inner peace in nirvana.

artificial description Conventionally held notions of things, which condition perceptions and experiences, and thus define the world as conceived by the socialized and acculturated mind.

Avalokiteshvara An archetypical bodhisattva or supernal enlightening being, representing redemptive compassion. Avalokiteshvara appears in many forms, according to context. Avalokiteshvara is associated with Amitabha Buddha. Often fancifully translated, the name Avalokiteshvara literally and technically means "the power of objective observation."

basic meditation See *four stages of meditation.*

Bhaishajyaguru "Master of Medicine," an archetypical supernal being, envisioned as a Buddha or a bodhisattva, representing healing.

birth and death "Samsara," the self-conditioning flow of changing thoughts, feelings, moods, mental states, and so on. Birth and death is often used to refer to bondage or delusion, or the context of bondage and delusion.

birthless A way of defining emptiness, *birthless* means that in the flow of interdependent conditioned events, discreteness of entities is defined by extrinsic characterization, not by intrinsic identity. When the conceptual faculty does not cling to objects as subjectively defined and does not reify them accordingly, with all the cognitive and emotive investment this implies, the freedom and fluidity that ensues is called birthlessness.

birthless reality The essential nature of things, which is so of itself and not by definition, which has no beginning or end, and which is not an appearance or an idea.

bodhisattva "Enlightening being," a broad category of Buddhist practitioners; those who strive for the welfare, liberation, and enlightenment of both self and others. Also used for archetypical supernal beings who represent specific qualities, properties, or virtues of Buddhahood.

Brahma A Hindu god, associated with the process of creation; also a class of gods, including several subclasses.

Brahman A hereditary Hindu intellectual or priest.

bronze wheel This "rank" of "rulership" represents the attainment of the ten abodes (q.v.).

Buddha-lands Spheres of influence of Buddhas; the outward reflections of the wisdom and compassion of Buddhas as they affect the external world.

Buddha-nature Defined in the *Mahaparinirvana-sutra* as being pure, blissful, permanent self, the Buddha-nature is also identified with true suchness and universal compassion; it is the "true self" in Buddhism.

Buddha of reward This refers to the Sambhogakaya, the body of reward, or perfect enjoyment, that is the psychological experience of an enlightened individual.

burning house A classical Buddhist metaphor (from the *Saddharmapundarika-sutra*, or *Lotus Scripture*) representing the world in view of its impermanence and instability.

celestial states Refined and elevated mental states attained through meditation and concentration.

cessation and contemplation Alternate terms for stopping and seeing.

Chou dynasty An ancient Chinese dynasty (1122–255 B.C.E.), era of famous philosophers such as Confucius and Lao-tzu.

Chudapanthaka A disciple of Gautama Buddha, said to be of extremely meager intellectual capacity, who nevertheless was able to attain arhatship, Buddhist sainthood, by a simple expedient devised by the Buddha. Descriptions of Chudapanthaka suggest that he may have been what is today termed mentally challenged, and his story is traditionally cited to illustrate that Buddhist liberation does not depend on sharpness of intellect in the conventional sense.

clusters Five components of sentient existence: form, sensation, perception, patterns of conditioning, and consciousness. The expression "five clusters" is often used to represent a mundane being.

common teaching The teaching of emptiness is called common because it is common to all vehicles of Buddhism, whether implicitly or explicitly.

conditional The conditional refers to all things. All relative existence is called conditional, in view of the fact that phenomena and beings invariably depend on a multitude of conditions for their existence.

Contemplation of Universal Good The final drama of the

Avatamsaka-sutra, or *Flower Ornament Scripture,* this contemplation presents an archetypical template of bodhisattva vows, or practical commitments.

delusions as numerous as dust particles and sand grains This technical term refers to particular or concrete instances or patterns of delusion, which are of indefinite number.

delusions of thought A general term for conceptual misconstructions of reality. Accurate thinking is part of the Buddha's path of liberation.

delusions of view A general term for misperception of reality. Accurate view is part of Buddha's path of liberation.

demon A general term for something that obstructs enlightenment. See *four demons.*

Dharma Flower Concentration A so-called repentance ceremony composed by Chih-i outlining a program of religious practice based on the *Lotus Sutra.*

dry wisdom Intellectual understanding without mental stabilization; also refers to contemplation of phenomena without realization of noumenon.

eight acceptances, or *eight recognitions* Four recognitions of truth and four associated recognitions. The four recognitions of truth are recognitions of suffering, its cause, its end, and the way to its end, in the context of the realm of desire. The four associated recognitions are recognitions of the foregoing truths in the contexts of the realm of form and the formless realm. These eight acceptances or recognitions correspond to the eight knowledges.

eight bodhisattvas Eight major archetypical enlightening beings, listed variously in different texts, including Avalokiteshvara, Manjushri, Akashagarbha, Vajrapani, Maitreya, Samantabhadra, Mahasthamaprapta, and Bhaishajyaguru. These images are used in devotional and meditational exercises.

eighteen unique qualities of Buddhas (1) Impeccability of action, (2) impeccability of speech, (3) impeccability of mind, (4) having no discriminatory thoughts, (5) unfailing concentration, (6) unfailing discernment and relinquishment, (7) endless volition, (8) endless vigor, (9) endless mindfulness, (10) endless wisdom, (11) endless liberation, (12) endless liberated knowledge and vision, (13) all actions according with knowledge and wisdom, (14) all speech according with knowledge and wisdom, (15) all thoughts according with knowledge and wisdom, (16) unobstructed insight into the past, (17) unobstructed insight into the future, (18) unobstructed insight into the present.

eighteen voids Eighteen aspects of emptiness: voidness of the internal, voidness of the external, voidness of both internal and external, voidness of voidness, voidness of magnitude, voidness of absolute truth, voidness of the compounded, voidness of the uncompounded, ultimate voidness, voidness of beginninglessness, voidness of dissolution, voidness of essence, voidness of identity, voidness of all things, voidness of ungraspability, voidness of nonexistent things, voidness of existent things, voidness of both nonexistent and existent things.

eightfold right path Right seeing, right thinking, right speaking, right action, right living, right effort, right mindfulness, right concentration.

eight forms (of fulfilling the Way) Archetypical stages in the life of a Buddha: descent from heaven into the womb, dwelling in the womb, birth on earth, living at home, leaving home, overcoming delusion and awakening, teaching others, passing away into final parinirvana.

eight knowledges See *eight acceptances.*

eight liberations Also-called *eight rejections*: (1) observation of external form with internal ideas of form, (2) observation of external form without internal ideas of form, (3) focus on purity, (4) focus on infinite space, (5) focus on infinite consciousness, (6) focus on nothingness, (7) focus on neither perception nor nonperception, (8) extinction of all sensation and perception.

eight recollections Also called *eight thoughts,* to be practiced when contemplation of impurity causes revulsion; these are eight points of remembrance, as follows: (1) Buddha, (2) Dharma, (3) harmonious communion, (4) morality, (5) relinquishment, (6) heaven, (7) breathing, (8) death.

eight rejections See *eight liberations.*

eight thoughts See *eight recollections.*

emanation bodies Physical embodiments of enlighten-ment, conceived as emanations or projections of Dharma as Truth and Reality.

fearlessnesses The four fearlessnesses of Buddhas are (1) confidence in true knowledge, (2) confidence in having ended spiritual pollution, (3) confidence in explaining obstacles, (4) confidence in explaining ways to end mis-ery. The four fearlessnesses of bodhisattvas are (1) confi-dence in retention and explanation of doctrines; (2) confidence in explaining doctrines with thorough knowl-edge of remedies, potentials, inclinations, and natures of people; (3) confidence in answering questions while ex-plaining doctrines; (4) confidence in ability to eliminate people's doubts in explaining doctrines.

five eyes The full spectrum of perception of Buddhas: (1) the corporeal eye, (2) the clairvoyant eye, (3) the eye of wisdom, (4) the eye of objective truth, (5) the eye of en-lightenment.

five faculties This refers to the "religious faculties" of faith, zeal, recollection, concentration, and insight. When fully developed, these are referred to as five powers, or five religious powers.

fivefold enlightenment Inspiration, subduing the mind, clarifying the mind, leaving mundanity for all-knowledge, attaining complete perfect enlightenment.

five hundred mental controls: Mental controls are concen-tration spells use to imbue the mind with certain princi-ples and control mental activity accordingly; the term is also used for states of mental mastery developed by spells or other methods of concentration. The number 500 is used in the *Great Treatise on Transcendent Wisdom,* supposed to refer to a minimum of an indefinitely large number of spells or mental controls.

five powers See *five faculties.*

five sins Crimes that bring immediate retribution: killing one's parents, breaking up a harmonious community, shedding a Buddha's blood, killing a saint, preventing religious initiation.

four bases of spiritual powers Bases of development of extraordinary psychic powers: intent, will, energy, and meditation.

four demons Demons refer to obstruction of enlightenment. The four demons are the demon of the mind-body clusters (form, sensation, perception, conditioning, and consciousness), the demon of afflictions, the demon of death, and the demon of heaven (which is in the realm of desire and thus blocks transmundane goodness).

four fruits of purification See *four stages of realization.*

four immeasurable minds Cultivated by bodhisattvas: a mind of infinite love, of infinite compassion, of infinite joy, and of infinite equanimity.

four integrative methods Means by which bodhisattvas integrate people into pure lands: generosity, kind speech, cooperation, and beneficial action.

four lands Realms of Buddhist experience: the land of common abode, where both ordinary and saintly live; the land of expediency, the realm of peaceful nirvana where saints live; the land of true reward, where bodhisattvas live; and the land of eternal silent light, the absolute realm of Buddhas.

four points of mindfulness Means of approaching nirvana: contemplation of the body as impure, of sensation as irritating, of mind as inconstant, and of phenomena as ungraspable.

four propositions The basic logical/experiential tetralemma, used to structure meditation: *(a)* is, *(b)* is not, *(c)* neither is nor is not, *(d)* both is and is not.

four qualities of the spiritual body Permanence, bliss, selfhood, and purity; these contrast with the impermanence, discomfort, inherent identitylessness, and impurity of the physical body.

four right efforts The effort to put a stop to unwholesome phenomena already arisen in mind, in speech, and in action; the effort to prevent such phenomena from arising in the future; the effort to foster wholesome phenomena in the mind, in speech, and in action; the effort to promote and develop wholesome phenomena already existing.

four stages of meditation Elementary meditation states, each traditionally defined as consisting of several elements, as follows: first, considering, examining, joy, bliss, single-mindedness; second, inner purity, joy, bliss, single-mindedness; third, equanimity, recollection, insight, bliss, single-mindedness; fourth, equanimity, neither pleasure nor pain, recollection, single-mindedness.

four stages of progress Stages of progress toward the four stages of realization (q.v.).

four stages of realization Four stages of attainment culminating in nirvana: Stream Entering, Once Returning, Nonreturning, and Arhat. Stream Entering is the initial entry into the Way. Once Returning means coming back to the ordinary world once before final liberation. Nonreturning means never coming back. Arhat means "worthy" or "killer of the enemy," and refers to saints in nirvana. These four stages are also called the four fruits of purification.

four truths There is suffering, suffering is caused, suffering has an end, there is a way to its end.

four universal vows The basic commitments of Mahayana Buddhism, by which it is oriented: the vow to liberate all beings, the vow to end all afflictions, the vow to study all truths, and the vow to fulfill enlightenment.

ghee A symbol of Buddha-nature, which is inherent in the human mind as ghee (clarified butter) is latent in milk.

Great Collection A collection of sutras (scriptures, or discourses attributed to Buddha). No complete Chinese translation exists, only a variety of partial translations done by a number of different translators.

Great Treatise The *Ta Chih Tu Lun,* or *Great Treatise on Transcendent Wisdom,* a commentary on the major *Prajnaparamita* scripture attributed to the great Buddhist writer Nagarjuna.

heroic progress concentration Surangama-samadhi in Sanskrit; said to be a state in which it is possible to enter progressively into all other states of concentration.

A Hundred Records of Clarification for the Nation A work by Chih-i's disciple Kuan-ting, who recorded *Stopping and Seeing*. The reference is thus the voice of the scribe.

interdependent origination The central principle that phenomena do not come into existence on their own but as a result of conditions. Nagarjuna identifies interdependent origination (*pratitya-samutpada*) with emptiness (*shunyata*).

Juan Chi A famous Chinese Taoist mystic eccentric, one of the Seven Sages of the Bamboo Grove.

Kapilavastu A city often mentioned in Buddhist scriptures as a site where Buddha taught.

lion-leap meditation This exercise is based on the nine stages of concentration (q.v.). It is twofold: "leaping in" and "leaping out." Instead of entering one stage of meditation in one session of practice, the practitioner enters and exits through the whole range of the nine stages. Using numerals to represent each stage, the structure of the lion leap meditation would be as follows: 1, 2, 3, 4, 5, 6, 7, 8, 9, 8, 7, 6, 5, 4, 3, 2, 1.

lion roar Symbolic of Buddha's teaching, especially the teaching of emptiness, which refutes all opinionated views, as illustrated in the saying "The roar of the lion bursts the brains of the jackals."

mahasattva A "great being," or bodhisattva ("enlightening being"), of the highest ranks.

Mahasthamaprapta A supernal bodhisattva representing knowledge and power.

Maitreya A supernal bodhisattva designated as the Buddha of the Future, representing a new world order based on loving-kindness.

major scripture This term refers to the major *Prajna-paramita-sutra*.

Manjushri A supernal bodhisattva representing wisdom and knowledge.

matrix of realization of thusness A term for Buddha-nature; also refers to the universe itself as the "mine" of understanding.

Nagarjuna A great Buddhist master and classical writer on emptiness; author of the *Verses on the Middle Way*. Considered an ancestor of Zen and Tantric Buddhism as well as T'ien-t'ai Buddhism.

Nanyue The teacher of Nanyue, or Nan-yueh, was meditation master Hui-ssu, who was the main teacher of Chih-i.

nine kinds of great meditation (1) Inherent meditation, (2) total meditation, (3) difficult meditation, (4) meditation providing entry into all meditations, (5) meditation of good people, (6) meditation including all practices, (7) meditation eliminating afflictions, (8) mediation bringing happiness in this world and the next, (9) pure clear meditation.

nine liberations The three realms (of desire, form, and formlessness) are each analyzed into three states, making nine states; the nine liberations refer to freedom from delusions of views and delusions of practice in each of these states.

nine nonobstructions Nonobstruction by the confusions of the nine states in the three realms; "nonobstruction" precedes "liberation." See *nine liberations.*

nine stages of concentration These consist of the four stages of meditation (q.v.), the four formless concentrations (infinite space, infinite consciousness, infinite nothingness, neither perception nor nonperception), and finally concentration in which all sensation and perception is quiescent. Also referred to as nine-step concentration.

nine thoughts Details of a practice of contemplating impurity in a corpse, or visualizing the decomposition of the body after death: (1) swelling, (2) discoloration, (3) decay, (4) blood, (5) pus, (6) being eaten by animals and birds, (7) disintegration of the skeleton, (8) a pile of bones, (9) bleached bones, or burned to ashes.

omni-science A technical term for ten powers of knowledge attributed to Buddhas as part of their total enlightenment: (1) knowledge of what is so and what is not, (2) knowledge of results of actions, (3) knowledge of all kinds of interests, (4) knowledge of all kinds of realms, (5) knowledge of different faculties, (6) knowledge of all destinations, (7) knowledge of all states of meditation and their associated techniques, (8) knowledge of past states, (9) knowledge of the conditions of death and birth of other beings, (10) knowledge of the end of contamination. Omni-science can also refer to universal knowledge (of the identity of relativity and emptiness), knowledge of all modes of methodology for enlightenment, and knowledge of all kinds of particulars.

one hundred and eight concentrations The total number of concentrations spoken of in the major scripture (q.v.) is reckoned to be one hundred and eight.

pith of a plantain A plantain tree has no pith, so the expression "the pith of a plantain" is used to refer to insubstantiality or absence of ultimate reality; transient phenomena are said to be "pithless as a plantain."

Prabhutaratna Buddha An important image in the *Lotus Scripture:* an ancient monument emerges from the ground, opens up, and reveals an extinct Buddha, named Prabhutaratna, who although extinct is still alive and teaching. This symbolizes the idea that truth is eternal, even though it may sometimes be concealed or forgotten, sometimes revealed or rediscovered.

raft In Mahayana Buddhism, the teaching is likened to a raft; when the goal, the Other Shore, is reached, then the raft is left behind. Similarly, according to the "metaphor of the raft," the teaching itself is relinquished when its end is attained. This means that the form of the teaching is not final dogma but expedient method.

rejections See *eight liberations.*

room, robe, and seat of Buddha The room of Buddha is compassion, the robe of Buddha is tolerance, and the seat of Buddha is the emptiness of all phenomena.

samsara "Birth and death," or conditional temporal existence; also means the arising and disappearance of thoughts in the stream of consciousness.

seven Buddhas Seven Buddhas of antiquity, the seventh being Shakyamuni, or Gautama Buddha, the historical Buddha. This is an illustration of the perennial nature of the Dharma or Truth realized by Buddhas, discovered and not invented by the historical Buddha.

seven elements of enlightenment Discernment, vigor, joy, ease, mindfulness, concentration, and equanimity.

seven expedient stages (1) The vehicle of humanity, (2) the vehicle of celestial states, (3) the vehicle of followers of Buddha, (4) the vehicle of the self-enlightened, (5) the vehicle of enlightening beings according to the Three Baskets teaching, (6) the vehicle of enlightening beings according to the common teaching, (7) the vehicle of enlightening beings according to the separate teaching.

seven ranks of sages (1) Practice according to faith, (2) practice according to principle, (3) confirmation, (4) perceptive attainment, (5) bodily realization, (6) liberation of intellect, (7) full liberation.

seven ranks of saints (1) Stabilizing the mind, (2) specific reflection, (3) general reflection, (4) warming, (5) peaking, (6) tolerance, (7) the highest state in the world.

Shakyamuni A name of the historical Buddha, Gautama.

Shariputra One of the great disciples of the historical Buddha, especially known for high intelligence; Shariputra often figures as an interlocutor in scripture.

six identities Six aspects or phases of identity of mind and Buddha-nature: (1) essential, (2) intellectual, (3) contemplative, (4) conformative, (5) partially realized, (6) wholly realized.

six perfections Basic parameters of the bodhisattva's path: (1) generosity, (2) morality, (3) tolerance, (4) perseverance, (5) meditation, (6) insight.

six spiritual powers Extraordinary capacities developed by arhats: (1) clairvoyance, (2) clairaudience, (3) mental telepathy, (4) psychic travel, (5) knowledge of past and future, (6) ending contamination.

six states of existence Representation of the totality of mundane conditional existence: (1) animals (symbolizing ignorance), (2) ghosts (greed), (3) titans (aggression), (4) hells (ignorance, greed, *and* aggression), (5) humanity (social virtue), (6) celestial states (meditational abstractions).

sixteen practices Based on the four truths—there is suffering, suffering is caused, suffering has an end, there is a way to its end. The sixteen practices consist of the acceptance and discernment of each truth and its types (i.e., types of suffering, causes, and so on).

sixteen truths The four truths on four levels: birth and death, birthlessness, the infinite, and the inconceivable.

ten abodes A schema of Buddhist practice and realization: (1) the abode of initial determination, (2) the abode of preparing the ground, (3) the abode of practical action, (4) the abode of noble birth, (5) the abode of fulfillment of skill in means, (6) the abode of the correct state of mind, (7) the abode of nonregression, (8) the abode of youthful nature, or innocence, (9) the abode of a prince of the teaching, (10) the abode of coronation. See the *Flower Ornament Scripture*, book fifteen, for a full description of these abodes.

ten dedications Dedications of Buddhas, which bodhisattvas vow to learn: (1) dedication to saving all sentient beings without any mental image of sentient beings; (2) indestructible dedication; (3) dedication equal to all Buddhas; (4) dedication reaching all places; (5) dedication of inexhaustible treasuries of virtue; (6) dedication causing all roots of goodness to endure; (7) dedication equally adapting to all sentient beings; (8) dedication with the character of true thusness; (9) unattached, unbound, liberated dedication: (10) boundless dedication equal to the cosmos. For a most detailed account of these dedications, see the *Flower Ornament Scripture*, book twenty-five.

ten epithets of Buddhas One Who Has Realized Thusness, Worthy, One with True and Universal Knowledge, Complete in Understanding and Action, Unexcelled in Understanding the World, Tamer of Humans, Teacher of Angels and Humans, Enlightened One, World Honored One.

ten evils Killing, stealing, raping, lying, divisive talk, harsh talk, suggestive talk, rage, false views.

ten powers See *omni-science*.

ten practices Ten bodhisattva practices: (1) the practice of giving joy, (2) beneficial practice, (3) the practice of nonopposition, (4) the practice of indomitability, (5) the practice of nonconfusion, (6) the practice of good manifestation, (7) the practice of nonattachment, (8) the practice of that which is difficult to attain, (9) the practice of good teachings, (10) the practice of truth. For details see the *Flower Ornament Scripture*, book twenty-one.

ten stages Ten stages of bodhisattvas: (1) extreme joy, (2) purity, (3) refulgence, (4) blazing, (5) difficult to conquer, (6) presence, (7) far-going, (8) immovability, (9) good mind, (10) cloud of teaching. For explanations of these stages, see the *Flower Ornament Scripture*, book twenty-six.

ten states of existence Ten states of being, which are inherent possibilities of the mind. These consist of the six states of existence (q.v.) plus the "holy" states of the saint, the self-enlightened, the bodhisattva, and the Buddha.

ten thoughts An exercise in detachment, contemplating

impermanence, suffering, selflessness, uncleanness of food, disinterest in the world, death, impurity, cessation, detachment, and exhaustion.

ten universes This refers to the *ten states of existence.*

thirty-seven elements of the path This term refers to the totality of the four points of mindfulness, the four right efforts, the four bases of spiritual powers, the five faculties, the five powers, the seven elements of enlightenment, and the eightfold right path. All of these individual sets are to be found in this glossary, and the elements of the path are more fully explained in the *Flower Ornament Scripture,* pp. 729–732.

three attributes Attributes of the spiritual body: liberation, wisdom, and reality.

three concentrations Absorption in the emptiness, signlessness, and wishlessness of all things in themselves.

three courses Affliction, compulsive action, suffering.

three doors of concentration Emptiness, signlessness, wishlessness.

three doors of liberation Same as three doors of concentration, but referred to in terms of results.

three emptinesses Also called three liberations: emptiness, signlessness, and wishlessness.

three eyes Perception of the three truths: absolute, conditional, and the Middle Way.

three knowledges Knowledge of, or in the modes of, the three truths; nondiscursive knowledge (of the absolute), discursive knowledge (of the conditional), and transcendental knowledge capable of perceiving the absolute and relative simultaneously.

three mires The states of ghosts, animals, and hells.

three obstacles Obstacles to enlightenment caused by afflictions (q.v.), actions, and consequences.

Three Treasures Buddha, Dharma, and Sangha; the Buddha, the Teaching, and the Community.

transcending meditation This exercise is based on the nine stages of concentration (q.v.). It is twofold, consisting of "transcending entry" and "transcending exit." The sense of "transcending" means passing over some stages in transcendent leaps from one stage to another. Assigning corresponding numerals to each of the nine stages, and assigning the variable x to the ordinary state of the scattered mind, the structure of the transcending meditation may be depicted as follows:
1, 8, 9, 1, 9, 2, 9, 3, 9, 4, 9, 5, 9, 6, 9, 7, 9, 8, 9, x, 9, x, 8, x, 7, x, 6, x, 5, x, 4, x, 3, x, 2, x, 1, x.

triplex world Also called the three realms, this world is pictured as consisting of a realm of desire, a realm of form, and a formless realm.

unfixed contemplation Meditation exercise that has different effects according to the spirit in which it is practiced; hence it is "unfixed" in terms of prescription and prognosis.

Vairochana Buddha   Representation of the cosmos as Buddha, or Adi-Buddha, "Primordial Buddha."

veils Phenomena that obstruct the mind from realization of truth in meditation: lust, anger, sleepiness, excitement and regret, and doubt.

Vimalakirti The main character in a popular Buddhist scripture named after him, Vimalakirti is a Buddha who is a householder, representing the realization of integration of the absolute and the relative. Vimalakirti is especially adept at undermining pseudoreligious attachments to limited doctrines and procedures.

Yu Wen   Name of the ruling house of the non-Chinese dynasty of Northern Chou in the mid–sixth century, under which Buddhism in northern China was subjected to a major purge.